ONLY ONE
STAR

ONLY ONE STAR

A Cure for the Celebrity Syndrome

DALE EVANS ROGERS

with Fritz Ridenour

WORD PUBLISHING
Dallas · London · Sydney · Singapore

Library of Congress Cataloging in Publication Data

Rogers, Dale Evans.
   Only one star.

   Includes bibliographical references.
    1. Christian life—1960-   2. Hero worship.
I. Ridenour, Fritz.   II. Title.
BV4501.2.R6413   1988   248.4   88-20527
ISBN 0-8499-0641-5

To my son
TOM
who introduced me
to the Real Star
forty years ago

Contents

Part I

What's Gone Wrong?

How and why celebrityism is reaping the whirlwind

1

Only One Star—
Only One Hope

This book has been growing within my soul for a long time. Having been in the entertainment industry for many years, I am well acquainted with the word "star," a term denoting someone who has made it in terms of success at his or her craft. When a person gains national or international recognition, he achieves "star status" and also enjoys the label "celebrity." Those who acquire star status and remain in that exalted position for a considerable time are then termed "super stars," whether they are in the entertainment industry, sports or any other competitive medium.

I have heard that the Christian church reflects society more than it transforms society. While I don't completely agree with that statement, I can see a lot of truth in it regarding stars and celebrities. Christians have their own star system and their own methods of recognizing "spiritual celebrities."

In recent years, long before the fall of the Bakkers, Jimmy Swaggart, and others, I have become increasingly concerned about the phenomenon called "celebrityism" and what it is doing to (not *for*) the cause of Christ.

The following incident, shared by Chuck Colson in his monthly Prison Fellowship newsletter, *Jubilee*, vividly captures my concern:

The red "on the air" light flashed, and the seventy-fifth interview of my *Kingdoms in Conflict* tour was under way. It felt like the seven hundred-fiftieth; for weeks I had been in and out of commercial television and radio stations across America, talking about church, state, and Christianity's role in public life.

At least I was getting a broad exposure to secular attitudes. It's good to leave our evangelical cocoons periodically and find out what people really think of us. But what I found was sobering—to say the least.

This day's session was typical. "Today we're interviewing Charles Colson," my host said smoothly. "But first, let's hear from 'God's little goof-balls.'" With that he flipped a switch, and a pre-recorded message from Jim and Tammy Bakker filled the studio. I'm not sure, but I think the inspiration recording included Tammy's recipe for three-layer bean dip. The interviewer grinned. "And now, we have another evangelist with us today. Let's hear what Chuck Colson has to say."

The majority of my nearly 100 interviews began in a similar manner. Christian-bashing is very much in fashion these days. The Bakker affair has produced a comic caricature of all Christians and derision that runs deeper than most of us realize.

At first I was defensive. But as the interviews continued I got angry. What about the 350,000 churches across America where people's needs are quietly being met? I asked. The thousands of missionaries to the poor, the army of Christian volunteers who faithfully go into prisons each week? Why do the media focus instead on the flamboyant few? It's not fair, I argued, to stereotype the whole church; we're not all hypocrites out to pad our own pockets.

But my interviewer simply smiled. Reason, after all, is no match for ridicule.[1]

Celebrityism Eats at Christianity's Vitals

I identify with Chuck Colson in his frustration because I've been there many times. Reason *is* no match for ridicule, particularly when the unbelieving world wants to ridicule Jesus Christ, Who from the beginning has laid claim to being the only Star worth following.

The title of this book is carefully chosen. There is only one Star, and His Name is Jesus. We believers, who supposedly number over fifty million in the United States alone, seem to have forgotten that. Celebrityism has eaten away at the vitals of Christianity for decades. But in the past fifteen to twenty years, "starmania" has taken over, especially through the medium of television. We have seen celebrities move into our living rooms to preach, teach, tell their life stories and give their opinions on just about every subject under the sun—plus a few from outer space.

I write these words realizing that I have been among those so-called celebrities who have invaded your living room from time to time. Along with my husband, Roy Rogers, I have spent most of my life on a stage and before microphones and cameras. We owe a great deal to media like films and television, and we like to think we have brought millions of people a lot of wholesome entertainment in return.

The church also has benefitted tremendously from films and even more so from television. Unquestionably, the cause of Christ has been advanced on screens both large and small across the world. The fault lies not in the tools of our trade but in how they are being used by those who achieve "stardom" as well as by fans and followers who let their admiration and appreciation spill over into false worship—in a word, *celebrityism*.

My purpose is not to bash Jim or Tammy Bakker or anyone else, but to have everyone think about how Satan is using celebrityism to further his ends. The devil misses no opportunities to attack the Kingdom of Christ. And what better way than through a medium that is capable of reaching the entire globe with a live broadcast at the same moment? Satan has always wanted to be the top star, shining more brilliantly than all the hosts of heaven, more brightly than God Himself. But God has reserved that right for His Son, Who is the Light of the world, the bright and morning Star.

The Morning Star Is Always There

Not long ago Roy set the alarm for me to arise well before daybreak to scan the skies of the waning night high above the upper desert of southern California, which has been our home for almost twenty-three years. I had been reading in Revelation about the bright morning Star, a reference to the power attached to Jesus Christ. And I wanted to see if there was, indeed, a star that fit the scriptural description.

Sure enough, I spotted it hanging in the clear winter skies just southeast of our home in Apple Valley. It was huge and it glittered brightly, thoroughly eclipsing all other stars in beauty and intensity. I had read somewhere that the morning star had spiritual significance because it heralds the coming light of day. After the prolonged darkness of night, the morning star is a welcome sight to many troubled and sleepless souls. But as I gazed at this star's brightness on that cold morning near my desert home, I thought of words from the very last chapter of the Bible. The Lord Himself spoke them through the revelation of St. John: ". . . I am the Root ánd the Offspring of David, the bright and Morning Star" (Rev. 22:16).

Jesus is the STAR of stars, King of kings, Very God of Very God. He has been my guiding Star since I was thirty-five years old. Before that I knew plenty about walking in the darkness and wanting the day to break. I grew more than a little weary with the world's "star system," and thank God, He freed me from all that.

Years ago there was a popular love song entitled "You're the Only Star in My Blue Heaven." I want to declare in no uncertain terms that Jesus Christ is the only real Star in my life! I have watched heroes who inspired me with their lives, screen personalities who delighted me with their performances, crusaders of noble causes who are worthy of acclaim—but the only real Star in time and eternity, for me, is Jesus Christ.

Several years ago Roy and I recorded a song called "Star of Hope." While it is a popular song not designed to speak directly of Jesus Christ, it is easy to see how the words can be applied to Him:

> Star of hope, star of love
> Shine down from afar.
> You're the one guiding light,
> No matter where we are.
>
> Through the valley of tears
> Through the long, weary years
> You're the star of faith, star of hope,

From heaven above.
Let each beam guide our dream
Leading to hope and love.[2]

Secular Media Suffer from Self-Inflicted Blindness

According to Marvin Olasky, a history of journalism professor at the University of Texas in Austin, ". . . until the mid-19th century, three quarters of America's magazines and newspapers were guided by Christian assumptions about life." Olasky observes, however, that today this is no longer true. For example, he refers to newspaper reports of the great Syrian earthquake of 1822. The *Boston Recorder,* New England's second largest newspaper, carried the headline: "Does it take an earthquake to turn us to God?"[3] You don't see headlines like that any more.

Writing in the "Speaking Out" Forum of *Christianity Today* magazine, David Aikman observes that the secular press has been missing "the scoop of the century" with its failure to observe, analyze and explain the tremendous increase in evangelical Christian faith across the world. Aikman calls it "one of the great modern blind spots of the American journalistic mind."

And who is David Aikman? A preacher who is out of sorts because he is being overlooked by the newspapers? A televangelist, perhaps, who would like a little more recognition? No, at the time his article appeared, David Aikman was a correspondent for *Time* magazine, covering the U.S. State Department.

Aikman speaks of the vague effort by the secular press to keep grassroots American evangelicals "out of sight and mind" by labeling them with that safe old standby, "fundamentalists." That word "fundamentalism," with its connotation of fanaticism, has the useful effect of consigning evangelicals to ". . . the category of the unreportable."[4]

That the secular media suffer from blindness is quite evident, but why? One explanation is ignorance, but it is a poor excuse. Some of the best reporting in history is being done by our leading daily newspapers. There must be another reason and surveys of the public media in the United States have unearthed it.

According to these studies, reporters for the press tend to be overwhelmingly secular in their world view. They don't respect religious faith, in general, and for the most part they have a system of values inherently hostile to the traditional Western values handed down in the Bible. One well-known survey of 216 leading journalists was conducted in 1981 by two sociologists, who discovered the following:

54 percent of the respondents thought adultery was not wrong.

75 percent considered homosexuality an acceptable lifestyle.

86 percent seldom or never went to church or synagogue.

90 percent thought abortion was an inherent right of women.[5]

Keep in mind that these were figures gathered seven years ago. Where are secular journalists today? It's doubtful that their values have swung toward Christianity. And as Aikman observes, "the recent string of scandals and internecine squabbles within the evangelical community" hasn't helped a bit.

Open hostility toward Christian organizations is often shown by news organizations in America. With a distinct lack of discernment (which should be a requisite skill for journalists!), they regularly tar much of Christendom with the same brush earned by only a small segment. This sad state of affairs was magnified and escalated by the scandals that made headlines throughout 1987 and 1988. As Philip Yancey said, "Tragically, the evangelicals who dominated the news in 1987 came across looking just like everybody else, only more so."[6]

Did Success Spoil Evangelicalism?

I don't think it is any coincidence that the advance of evangelical Christianity and the Kingdom of Christ in the United States and around the world has happened at unprecedented rates in the last two decades—decades marked by the use of television, radio and films. But this advance has also brought its dangers.

Back in June of 1986 there was a gathering of Christian leaders sponsored by Eastern College and Eastern Baptist Theological Seminary at St. Davids, Pennsylvania. The topic of their three-day discussion was "Evangelicalism: Surviving Its Success." Many excellent speakers shared their thoughts, but the most telling speech was offered by Dr. Roberta Hestenes. She compared the church at Corinth to present-day evangelicalism as she warned against the perils of "success."

Dr. Hestenes specifically admonished the church concerning the seduction of success, superstar mentality and the problem of superficiality. Hestenes charged that some evangelicals were becoming confused about means and ends and were getting so hooked on success they were employing the wrong means to advance the Kingdom. She talked about contemporary evangelical leadership being characterized by glamorous personalities rather than by intellectual or even spiritual giants. Further, she discussed the concurrent pivotal problem of lack of accountability.

"There is always the danger," cautioned Hestenes, "that charismatic leaders tend to equate themselves with God. To challenge them is to challenge God."[7] With the Bakker scandal less than a year away, Dr. Hestenes' words were prophetic, to say the least.

Other warnings had been voiced even earlier. The Reverend Billy Graham, whom Ted Engstrom calls "the most respected evangelist of our time," had appeared in press conferences and interviews on different occasions in the early 1980s, warning that televangelists should avoid excesses in appealing for money and should curb the stress of on-camera emotionalism. Engstrom writes: "In a March 1983 *TV Guide* cover story, Dr. Graham warned of the dangers of mixing money and politics with televised religion. An opponent of heavy-handed tactics for raising money from television viewers, Graham founded the Evangelical Council for Financial Accountability (ECFA) to promote annual audits and open financial records."[8]

Billy Graham has always bent over backwards to avoid the slightest appearance of any suggestion of fraud or misuse of funds. Years ago, for example, his organization stopped appealing to viewers for "love offerings." All Graham Crusade financial statements are open to public scrutiny.

In his book, *Integrity*, Engstrom estimates that more than

107 million people have heard Billy Graham since his first crusade in 1947. He has preached to more people in person than anyone else in history. On two different occasions in Seoul, Korea, he spoke to one million people attending a single day's session. He has held crusades in forty-six states and sixty-four countries. By the end of 1987, he had planned to complete a crusade circuit in all fifty states.

According to Dr. Engstrom, the Graham family lives in a modest North Carolina mountain home. Now in his late 60s, Graham and his wife, Ruth, have five children and eighteen grandchildren. He drives a 1977 Oldsmobile and his current salary, set by the Billy Graham Evangelistic Association board, is $69,000 a year. Billy Graham never takes any "cut" from a local crusade committee. All money raised through his ministry goes directly into the BGEA to support its evangelism programs.[9]

I have visited Billy's comfortable, but definitely not lavish, home in Montreat and recall how his wife, Ruth, bustled about the kitchen serving us coffee and doughnuts. I remember being particularly impressed with how Billy had not let "success and fame" affect his lifestyle and, most importantly, his attitude toward money and things. Unfortunately, though, secular TV talk show hosts and journalists don't make headline stories out of facts like these. Exorbitant salaries, sexual misconduct, air-conditioned dog houses and shopping sprees make much better grist for their mills.

That One Ray of Hope in the Darkness

It is now painfully obvious that the warnings by people like Billy Graham and Roberta Hestenes were not heeded. Now the secular press thinks it has more reason than ever to condemn evangelicals, not only to the ranks of "fundamentalist fanatics" but as phonies and hypocrites as well. But in all the mess, there is one bright ray of hope. Evangelical journalist Cal Thomas writes a syndicated column published in many secular newspapers throughout this country. According to Thomas, his friends in the secular media think the scandals surrounding Jim Bakker and Jimmy Swaggart mean one of two things:

1. All evangelicals are hypocrites.

2. Or, perhaps they—the secular journalists—should pay more attention to the claims of Christianity for the same reason that the Bakkers and the Swaggarts have been called to account. According to Thomas, some of these journalists are getting the message that "God humbles the proud and makes accountable those who speak in his name."[10]

I say "Amen" to that. God does humble the proud and He does call us all to account. There is an old saying, "Don't curse the darkness; light a candle." I want to do much more than that. I want to point to the Light Who has always held darkness and chaos at bay —Jesus Christ, the bright and morning Star. Today Satan is trying to eclipse His light by subtly luring Christians into thinking that *their* "stars" are shining brightly and guiding people on the right path. Unfortunately, some of these stars are leading people astray.

As never before in the history of the church, we must follow more closely the only true Star, the living Word of God, Who has been there from the beginning. As John wrote in his Gospel, "Through him all things were made; without him nothing was made that has been made. In him was life, and that life was the light of men. The light shines in the darkness, but the darkness has not understood [or overcome] it" (John 1:3–5).

In his wonderful translation, J. B. Phillips has John 1:5 read: "The light still shines in the darkness and the darkness has never put it out."

The darkness of unbelief and denial of the incarnation of God in the Person of Jesus Christ have tried to put out His light for centuries. Unbelief is still desperately trying to extinguish the light of the bright and morning Star, but to no avail. For Jesus Himself said, "Heaven and earth will pass away, but my words will never pass away" (Matt. 24:35).

At this critical time in church history, many of us can gather our righteous skirts about us, point fingers and wag our heads in dismay over the mistakes of a few. But it will be more useful and beneficial to confess our own pride and focus on our own accountability. We all need to think about what star we really follow, and that is precisely what I want to talk about in the following chapters.

2

What Star Do
We Follow?

Recently I got a letter from my granddaughter, Mindy, who has served with Youth With A Mission in Amsterdam, Holland, for the past seven years. She is married to Jon Petersen and they are rearing three children while living on the typically sacrificial missionary income. Mindy's letter began:

> Dear Grandma Dale,
> I came across this article the other day and was reminded of the book you are currently writing. May this be an encouragement to you to *press on* with what is on your heart. It *does* need to be said! We are all so sadly aware of the pitfalls of notoriety at this moment in the history of "evangelicalism." A wonderful Christian leader from New Zealand challenged YWAM a while back: "You've been tested over the years by living simply—doing your work as one of the largest missionary organizations with very little recognition. But your greatest test is to come. The test of *notoriety.*" It was a sobering word and one that we take *very seriously!*

The clipping Mindy enclosed was one written by Karen Burton Mains, who has written many fine devotional books, including *Open Heart—Open Home, With My Whole Heart,* and *Making Sunday Special.* Karen's regular column in *Today's Christian Woman* opened with a line from Anne Morrow Lindbergh,

wife of the legendary Charles Lindbergh, first man to fly the
Atlantic alone and make it. Mrs. Lindbergh, who obviously knew
something about the burdens of being made a celebrity, once
confided: "Fame is a kind of death . . . ."

Karen Mains went on to observe that for Christians in public
ministry, fame can lead to a kind of spiritual death. She recalled
being one of several speakers at a women's retreat. She heard
someone say, "Oh, the celebrities are here!" A wave of revulsion
swept over her and she vowed then and there ". . . never to forget that in the Kingdom there is only one *Persona*, Christ! There is
only one *Celebrity*, Christ; there is only one *Star*, this One."[1]

Name Recognition Is the Celebrity Game

In case you're curious, I didn't get the title of this book from
Karen's statement. But I couldn't agree with her more. In her
article she honestly confronted the all too real tendency of Christians to mimic the worship of stars that is done as a matter of
course in the secular world. Whether we want to admit it or not,
we Christians operate by the same standard that controls secular
thinking: *name recognition*. Like everyone else, Christians take
advantage of name recognition to purchase the best air time on
radio or TV. Christian publishers want to do your book because
your name is known. Name recognition, admitted Karen, is what
got her picture on the cover of the magazine in which her article
appeared—*Today's Christian Woman*. She continued:

> Name recognition tempts those of us who are on the
> "Christian speakers' circuit" to think more highly of ourselves
> than we ought, to become convinced that our gifts of speaking
> and writing are somehow qualitatively more important than those
> of the most unknown Christian in the body. We begin to believe
> the publicists' press releases. A *persona* begins to emerge, not our
> real human selves. We are one person at home, but something else
> in public—a creature who performs, a myth. . . . We are ap-
> palled by the fall of Christian leaders, casualties often of a public
> ministry. But I am even more appalled by the temptation to err I
> discover in my own heart. I have often been like a friend who
> candidly confessed, "I want it so bad I can taste it!"[2]

I Wanted Stardom from Age Three On

I know the feeling of wanting recognition Karen shares so honestly. In fact, I have known it practically all my life, which began when I was born Frances Octavia Smith on October 31, 1912. At age three I decided to make my "gospel solo debut" one Sunday morning in our little Baptist church in Italy, Texas. While the congregation was zestfully singing a lively hymn, I decided to dance down the aisle, swishing my skirts and singing as loudly as the rest. Instead of stardom, though, all it got me was a spanking.

Later, when my little brother, Hillman, was born, I got so put out with his celebrity status as the "new baby" that I ran away from home—all the way to the pigpen out back, where I sat in the mud and had a genuine pity party with a newborn litter of pigs. Fortunately, my maternal grandmother saw what had happened and called my dad, who plucked me out of what might have been real danger. Sows with babies are not known for being friendly.

Always impulsive, I continually pushed myself hard. I entered school at age seven and kept skipping grades until I arrived in eighth grade at age eleven. But trying to keep up with all those older kids didn't bring me celebrity status. Instead, I had a nervous breakdown that kept me in bed for an entire summer vacation. My mother often said I never did anything at normal speed. For me, it was full throttle or nothing.

I took piano lessons because of musical aptitude, but my teacher soon gave up on me. Right in the middle of a lesson one afternoon, she told my mother, "Mrs. Smith, I'm wasting my time and your money. Your daughter is too much of an improviser to learn to play properly. She won't practice the scales or the pieces I assign to her."

And she was right. Because I hated the routine of running up and down scales, I spent practice time "improvising" my own compositions. After losing my piano teacher, I learned to play by ear the kind of songs I liked and could sing best.

My parents were very devout, and I regularly attended church with them—but with motives that were more social than spiritual! When I was ten, our church held a revival, and I recall walking the

aisle more out of fear of hell-fire and eternal darkness than any real
faith in Christ. The real faith was to come much later, after I had
made my share of mistakes in my quest for fame and stardom.

I Did a "Load of Compromisin'"

Glen Campbell's hit song of the 1970s describes my first
thirty years to a "T." One of the lines in "A Rhinestone Cowboy"
talks about all the "compromisin'" we do on the way to fulfilling
our dreams, "the lights . . . shining on me."

And I tried for those lights—oh, how I tried, always sure I
could handle my life my way and make my own decisions. Unfortunately, I made a lot of bad choices, all of which are recorded in
Happy Trails,[3] a book Roy and I wrote together in 1979.

At fourteen I ran away and married my high school boy-
friend. A year later he left me and I had his child, whom I named
Thomas Frederick Fox, Jr. My first husband's goodbye note mentioned needing freedom and being too young to be tied down to a
wife and child. I was too young to be tied down to a child too, but
heartbroken as I was, I swore I would never give up little Tommy,
even when Mother suggested adoption.

I lashed out in all directions and only hurt myself and others. Emotionally, I was immature, insecure and totally selfish. I
tried as best I could to rationalize my feelings of guilt and failure.
I learned typing and shorthand and took various secretarial jobs,
but my real interest was in the creative—I still wanted to be a star.

For awhile I tried writing short stories and some song writing, all with no success. Later I got a start singing on radio stations
in Memphis. Finally, during the Depression, I went to Chicago,
where I could find no radio work. Literally, I almost starved to
death on a secretary's meager wages and had to wire Mom and
Dad for money to get back home.

Although it took several months to regain my health, I
never gave up on chasing stardom and having those bright lights
shine on me. In 1935 I caught on as a vocalist with a Louisville,
Kentucky, radio station, and it was there that I took my stage
name, Dale Evans.

Things were finally looking up—until the day Tom became deathly ill with what looked like polio. While doctors examined him I made all kinds of rash promises to God: "Lord, if You will see to it that these tests turn out negative, I'll do anything You want me to do. I'll forget about show business. I'll read my Bible every day and I'll pray and be faithful to You. I promise to put You first in my life."

The tests turned out negative, but so did my wonderful promises to God. They lasted about two weeks. Following my short-lived commitment, I moved back to Texas and sang for a Dallas radio station, leaving Tom with my mother at the farm during the week. Being a slow learner, I remarried—this time to a man named R. Dale Butts, a composer and pianist.

From Dallas our small family moved to Chicago, where I took vocalist jobs in hotels and supper clubs. All the while, R. Dale worked as a composer/arranger at NBC. Although our hectic schedules left us barely enough time to say "hello" and "goodbye," I did spend all the time I could with Tom, by then a junior high school student.

Ironically, I always made sure we attended church regularly because I wanted Tom to have a solid grounding in the Christian faith. What I didn't realize was that I was the one who needed a real faith in Christ, but that would come later. At the time I thought I was doing pretty well. I was making enough money to think about sending Tom to college and was even gaining a certain amount of the fame I had always thirsted for besides. For a little country gal from Texas, I wasn't doing badly at all.

Hollywood Called and I Finally Answered

When a wire arrived from a Hollywood agent who had heard me sing over the radio, I laughed off his request for photographs. As badly as I wanted stardom, I doubted I was Hollywood material. Soon, though, a second wire came and I decided to send some photos. What did I have to lose? After a few more weeks, a third wire arrived saying, "Come at once." I went out to Hollywood, took a screen test and got a one-year contract with Twentieth Century Fox at three times the salary I had made at the radio station. R. Dale thought it was a great idea for all of us to move to California. What better place for a composer/arranger than Hollywood?

My son had other reactions. What bothered him most was the little "catch" that I had to tell him about. To become a movie star, I had to agree to my agent's unwavering demand to tell people that Tom was my little brother, not my son. There simply was no room for twenty-eight-year-old mothers of twelve-year-olds among Hollywood starlets at that time.

After one year in Tinseltown, I had done two walk-on parts and spent a lot of time with the drama coach. Twentieth Century Fox chose not to renew my contract and when my agent entered the military service, he recommended a man named Art Rush. Art liked my singing and got me a job with the Chase and Sanborn Hour, starring Edgar Bergen and Charlie McCarthy. Don Ameche was a vocalist on the show, which also featured Ray Noble and his orchestra, one of the great "big bands" of the time.

Singing on the Chase and Sanborn Hour was one of the great thrills of my career to that point. It also proved to be one of the most petrifying experiences I ever had. Working with all those celebrities totally intimidated me. I got such severe stage fright my knees literally knocked. My goal had been doing musicals on the New York stage or on a coast-to-coast radio show, just like the Chase and Sanborn Hour. When I finally achieved my dream, however, I almost panicked.

But all in all, my star seemed to be on the rise. The one fly in the ointment was still having to lie about Tom being my brother instead of my son. He and I attended Hollywood First Baptist and the minister's sermons started to get to me, especially the one about people with God-given musical talent who refused to honor the Lord by putting those gifts to use in the church. Although Tom said nothing, I knew what he was thinking.

I "Go Thataway" to Stardom

My job with Chase and Sanborn lasted until 1943 but my option wasn't renewed. I counted on Art Rush to find me something else, but at the time he seemed more than a little preoccupied with other clients like Nelson Eddy and a singing cowboy named Roy Rogers. I did a slow burn while all Art seemed to be able to do was talk about Roy and run off to schedule more appearances for him. Finally I told Art that since he didn't seem to have time for me, perhaps we had better go our separate ways.

I found a new agent and soon had a new contract with Republic Pictures. I worked on eight different films that first year and also toured army bases, where I did shows and benefits.

While visiting my parents in Texas, I got a call saying, "Get back to Hollywood immediately." The owner of Republic Pictures had a new offer—the female lead in Roy Rogers westerns! It was hardly the stuff of which my dreams of classy musicals had been made, but with my ego smarting, I did four westerns with Roy that next year. Academy Award winners they weren't, but when fan mail started coming in addressed to Dale Evans, I decided that riding around on horses and delivering lines like "He went that-away" might not be so bad after all.

Back then, in the 1940s, Roy Rogers was a celebrity, but he never gave in to the myth or acted like a star. And working with him was far more enjoyable than I had ever thought possible. In fact, he was the most giving person I'd ever met. A devoted family man, he was forever talking about his wife and two daughters. He loved spending time with kids, and his devotion to children wasn't any celebrity put-on. He was totally unaffected, very down-to-earth, and not the least bit phony.

As for me, I was having a little more trouble with being a phony. Tom was graduating from high school that year and I still maintained my masquerade as his older sister, a deception that ate at me constantly.

I attended Tom's graduation disguised with no makeup, a different hairdo, dark glasses and my plainest dress. I sat there virtually incommunicado, unable to share with anyone that it was my son up there, conducting the school orchestra in a piece he had both written and arranged.

My Hunger for Stardom Led to a Divorce

The rest of my family life hadn't done that well either. Due to our careers, R. Dale and I seldom saw each other and had no real life together. I let my hunger for stardom and celebrity status take over my life and send me in an opposite direction that led to divorce.

After nine more westerns, I had all I wanted of hayseed, homilies, fistfighting and shootouts. I also disliked fourth billing. All the promo read the same: "Starring Roy Rogers and Trigger, Gabby Hayes and Dale Evans."

I made waves for the studio, threatened to quit and once told a newspaper reporter, "A heroine in a western is always second string. The cowboy and his horse always come first."

In 1947 my contract with Republic ended and so did my career as a cowgirl—or so I thought. I did radio for awhile, as featured singer with Jimmy Durante and Garry Moore on their network show. Then I got an offer from RKO to do a musical starring Eddie Cantor and Joan Davis. But after a long wait, that project was shelved and I got a call from Mr. Yates of Republic Studios. "You might as well come back and get on a horse where you belong," he invited. And do you know everybody—Roy, Gabby Hayes, The Sons of the Pioneers, even Trigger—welcomed me warmly! It was as if I had never left.

Although we were opposite in temperament, Roy and I became friends. We had long talks and shared problems with each other. His wife had died suddenly a year before. I even shared with Roy my frustration about masquerading as Tom's sister instead of telling the world I was his mother.

Roy Proposed to Me on Horseback

While Roy and I were on a promotional tour together, he proposed in the most unlikely setting—as we sat astride our horses in the chutes of massive Chicago Stadium, waiting to do our act. We were married the following New Year's Eve and I settled down trying to build a home for our "Brady Bunch"— Roy's two daughters, Linda Lou and Cheryl, and his baby son, Dusty. My own Tom was twenty at the time and attending the University of Southern California.

For the time being I had to drop out of picture-making, a decision which seemed to suit Republic Studios fine. They

weren't sure how Roy's marriage would go over with his fans
and were content not to have his wife appear on the screen with
him as a constant reminder of something they wanted all
moviegoers to forget.

Retiring from pictures was okay with me. Besides, I had my
hands full trying to learn the role of stepmother, which wasn't
easy. Roy's daughters resented me as an intruder and let me know
I could never replace their mother. While I understood that, it
didn't make it any easier.

My own son, Tom, encouraged me to try taking everyone to
church. We attended Fountain Avenue Baptist Church on the following Sunday, and Dr. MacArthur's sermon, "The House That Is
Built on a Rock of Faith," seemed pointed straight at me. When an
invitation was extended, I almost went down front but decided to
postpone my decision for a couple of weeks. I needed time to think.

I went home to a quiet house. Roy was away on a hunting
trip and I went up to my room, got on my knees to pray and cry
—and pray and cry some more. I went over my life and my
perpetual desire to be a star and a celebrity.

I could see that there was a huge chunk of something missing. Tom had been so perceptive. He knew I didn't really know
Christ as my Lord. Oh, I had made sure we had gone to church
and I talked about faith but I didn't really have much. Right there
I asked God's forgiveness and promised that the following Sunday I'd be the first person down that aisle.

And I was. That day was the most glorious of my whole life.
An indescribable peace flowed into me and I experienced joy I
had never known before.

"Evans, You're Just Not the Same . . . ."

My new faith in the Lord had its ups and downs. There
weren't any overnight miracles with the girls, but tension did ease
as we read Bible stories together and got better acquainted. At a
party we threw to celebrate the completion of another picture by
Roy, I was confronted by one of his leading ladies, "Evans, what
has happened to you? You're just not the same . .   "

When I tried to explain that I had a different perspective and realized I had new responsibilities with my marriage and three stepchildren, Roy overheard and misunderstood. He bluntly told me, right in front of the leading lady, "If you have a problem, this is no place to talk about it." Then he walked away. The rest of the evening was difficult and, as I went to bed, there was strained silence between us. Roy was still standing at the window staring into the night as I fell asleep.

But the next morning—a Sunday—I was getting ready to take the children to Sunday school and church when Roy said, "If you're going to church tonight, I'm going with you."

And he did accompany me to the evening service. I didn't think he heard much at all during the sermon—he seemed asleep —but when the invitation was given, he sat bolt upright, turned to me and said, "Mama, I'm going down there." And he did just that—he accepted Jesus Christ as his Savior!

A week later Cheryl accepted Christ too, and she and her dad were baptized on the following Palm Sunday. My cup of joy was running over and then some. The spiritual bond formed in our family that day has remained strong through the years. More important, that bond has given us strength to cope with tragedy as well as success. The deaths of three of our children are shared in our book, *Happy Trails*.

Tragedy Protected Us from Our Own Success

When Robin, the only child born to Roy and me, died of congenital heart disease, I thought I'd had my share of grief. A Down's syndrome baby, Robin had drawn our family together, strengthened all of us spiritually and filled us with love and compassion for others. In *Angel Unaware*, I told Robin's story from her point of view, as she might have shared it with her Heavenly Father. This book sold more than 1,300,000 copies and is still selling today.

But our tragedies didn't end with Robin. Our adopted son, Sandy, and our adopted daughter, Debbi, were also taken in heartbreaking circumstances. As tragedies often do, the children's untimely deaths and our pain kept our perspective clear and protected us from our own success.

From the 1950s on, Roy and I had every opportunity to succumb to the lure of celebrityism. In the years immediately following our marriage, Roy became the number one western box-office star, a position he held for twelve consecutive years. I teamed with him in twenty-eight of the eighty-seven musical westerns he made for Republic. And after "retiring" from films following our marriage, I continued to make appearances with him at rodeos and other shows.

Art Rush, who had remained Roy's agent and became mine again, took full advantage of a clause in Roy's contract that gave him rights to his name, voice and likeness for any commercial endeavors. Roy Rogers products, including charm bracelets, neckerchiefs, toy guns, lariats, clothing and games, flooded America. In addition, millions of Roy Rogers comic books were bought by his young fans and four Roy Rogers novels were published annually for several years. Roy Rogers song books were also a hot item. Roy Rogers fan clubs grew to over five million members, with two thousand clubs operating in the United States and one chapter in London reporting a membership of fifty thousand. It was the largest individual fan club in the world.

Quaker Oats sponsored a Roy Rogers radio show weekly, and by the mid-fifties Roy and I had branched out into television. General Foods sponsored us on TV for six and one-half years in more than a hundred half-hour adventures.

Roy and I have been on many television specials and spectaculars and made more than a hundred guest appearances, as well as more than a hundred commercials. We have received more awards than we can count. One of my favorites is "Texas Woman of the Year," which I received in 1970 from the Press Association in my native state.

Roy has appeared on the covers of *Life* and *Time* magazines, and both of us were on the cover of *The Saturday Evening Post*. When Ralph Edwards did a "This Is Your Life" program on Roy, he told us he had more requests to do Roy's life than any other person in the world. That show has been repeated three times by popular demand.

We Understand the Temptations of Stardom

That only scratches the surface. I could list many other awards, achievements, honors and examples of "stardom." I don't tell you this to boast, but to let you know Roy and I have tasted what many call "real success," and we understand the temptations that come with it. True success for the Christian, however, is becoming all that God has in mind for you to be. And our greatest blessing has been watching God work in us to will and to do of His good pleasure, not ours. I can honestly say that neither Roy nor I have ever been impressed by our achievements in the enter-tainment field. Thankful, yes, but impressed with ourselves, no. In fact, Roy has often said, "How I ever got into show business, I'll never know, unless God had it in mind."

My "thirst for stardom" has been more than satisfied, but only after Christ became the real Star of my life. When He came in I changed. Not totally, but fundamentally, I became a different person. When I gave my life to the Lord, I realized I wasn't any-thing, except what He chose to be in me. I didn't become perfect, I still had a big ego, but gave that to Him too. And He knows count-less ways to keep it under control!

The first thing Christ did for me after I had walked the aisle in Jack MacArthur's church was take away my stage fright and insecurity. In the past, when another performer was more attrac-tive, had a better voice or got a bigger hand, I felt very threatened and insecure. When I had performed on the Chase and Sanborn Hour, for instance, it hit me that I had finally "done it." I was elated to be a singer on such an important program. But when I listened to a recording after one of my first shows, all I heard were the sharp and flat notes. I was my own worst critic and constantly had to battle depression.

After Christ became my best Friend, however, He showed me I didn't have to be afraid or insecure because He would use whatever abilities or talent I had to entertain people in a wholesome way for His glory. When I realized that, it took all the pressure off. I soon reached the point where hitting a sour note didn't destroy me the way it used to. I still try to do my best, but if it doesn't always work out, I don't take it personally.

Keep Quiet about Christ? Never!

Another thing Christ gave Roy and me was the courage never to back away from opportunities to speak a word for Him. In 1954, for example, we were invited to make personal appearances in England. It was perfect timing because Billy Graham was planning to hold his first crusade in that country and we were asked to give our testimony in his meetings.

We went to England six weeks ahead of Billy and appeared in stage shows in Glasgow, Edinburgh, Manchester, Liverpool, Belfast and Dublin. We took Trigger and did our entire western show, which always included a salute to God and country at the end. The man who booked us called Art Rush and told him to instruct me to keep quiet about the Bible and most certainly not to mention Billy Graham's coming to England. "We haven't hired her to preach over here," he warned.

Well, I didn't see it as preaching at all, but he took it that way. Furthermore, I certainly didn't intend to be quiet about Billy Graham. While I didn't plan to be his press agent, I didn't plan to avoid mentioning him either.

Crowds came in unbelievable numbers. People almost tipped over our car. They grabbed at our clothing and tried to pull the fringes off of our shirts and jackets—anything for a souvenir.

In a crushing crowd in Belfast, Ireland, I saw a woman drop her baby when she tried to get close enough to look at us. Somehow she managed to scoop up the child before it was trampled to death. I got hysterical watching. It was just after we had lost our little Robin.

All that attention was heavy to bear. I was caught between being tempted to think I was really that important and being turned off by all the glittery glory.

I found peace in the thought that as long as I was a committed Christian and all these people had this much interest and affection, why not use it to draw them to see what makes me tick? I like drawing crowds, adulation and praise as much as anyone, but what I really want to do is point people to the Lord, not to Dale Rogers.

"What Kind of a Man Is Billy Graham?"

I remember being backstage at Glasgow in 1954. Our dressing rooms were on the second floor, with a balcony that looked out over an entire city block. One cold, misty day the street became solid with people in back of the theatre (somebody had told them where our dressing room was). "We want Roy, we want Dale, we want Roy," the crowd kept chanting.

Finally we had to go out on the balcony and wave and try to sing a chorus of "Happy Trails" with no mike. The crowd loved it and we both wound up with European flu!

Billy was due to arrive soon, and we were scheduled to spend eight days with him in his crusade meetings. I remember reading scathing articles about him in the English press and becoming so furious I wanted to butt my head against the wall. All the while, the man who had booked us kept warning me, "Hush up about Billy Graham. Don't you read the newspapers?"

Yes, I had read the newspapers and saw how they were denigrating one of God's real servants. But I refused to be quiet.

When Roy and I went to Ireland for an appearance in Belfast on St. Patrick's Day, the booking agent cautioned, "You tell Dale and Roy if they talk about the Bible or about Billy Graham, these people will throw rotten vegetables at them."

All I said was, "Well, okay, so be it."

We gave the show and said our piece about God and country —and Billy. It was the only place in the British Isles where we received a standing ovation!

In the wings a Catholic monk, dressed in robe and sandals, complete with the rope around his middle, watched Roy and me.

He sent word, "I want to talk to Dale Evans." I went over to him
and thought, *Oh, dear, he's really going to get on me for what I've
said—this is solid Irish Catholic territory.*

Instead, the monk said simply, "I want to ask you a very
personal question. I don't want to embarrass you, but what kind
of a man is Billy Graham?"

"Sir," I replied, "he is the most utterly committed Christian
I have ever met in my life."

The monk said to me, "I knew it. Will you tell him I said,
'God bless his ministry'?"

I've never shared that story before, but here is an example of
how all of us, no matter what our denomination, can worship
Him—the pivotal One, the bright and morning Star Himself,
Jesus Christ.

Romans 8:28 Really Does Work

I've shared some of my life and struggles with you in this
chapter for one reason—to demonstrate that Romans 8:28 does
work: "And we know that all things work together for good to
them that love God, to them who are the called according to his
purpose" (KJV). After a sad beginning in which I was intensely
preoccupied with becoming a star and successful celebrity, my
career in radio, films, and television has ultimately worked for
good.

For my first thirty-five years I hitched my wagon to a star of
success. My ego was totally in control and led to lots of bad
scenes. There were many things I wanted and struggled to attain
under my own steam and through my own power. When I
finally gave my desires to God, though, I was able to say, "Okay, if
You want it for me, God, then it's fine; but if You don't want it,
that's fine too." Then and only then, many of the things I de-
sired were given to me.

As I have said before, "When we are able to submit ourselves
to God and ask Him through Christ to use us, our priorities start
to fall in place. We begin to listen to the leading of His Holy Spirit
instead of to our egocentric wishes."[5]

Discipleship—following Christ wherever He leads—centers on wanting His will, His guidance and His control over our lives. Celebrityism—making those who have been created more important than their Creator—centers on "I, me and mine." In the next chapter I want to take a closer look at this phenomenon called celebrityism and identify a few of the many dangers in star gazing.

3

Dangers of Star Gazing

Why are you—a celebrity—criticizing celebrities?"

I've been asked that question several times while working on this book. It's a good question, because it gets to the very heart of what *Only One Star* is all about.

In the first place, I am not criticizing actors, speakers, evangelists, musicians or athletes, per se. All these professions often achieve the fame that begets the label "celebrity." But I am deeply concerned about the dangers of *celebrityism*, which I define as putting mere human beings on some kind of pedestal that raises them to a level of importance not only wrong but dangerous.

In the second place, I dislike and reject the label "celebrity" and do everything I can to discount it. The star system of the world does not awe me. I do not consider myself a star and care nothing for status. I only want to express myself with all the ability God has given me.

Because I've been in the motion picture business much of my life, I have seen firsthand how the star system controls so many people. Before I left Chicago for that first screen test in Hollywood in 1941, a character actress on the radio "soaps" took me aside and said: "In Hollywood, the people who really make it and survive are the ones who do not believe their publicity. They are the ones who remember who they were when they came.

36

They establish a comfortable lifestyle and hold to it. They do not get mixed up in their personal lives. When they are invited to a Hollywood party, they arrive late and leave early. If they are early, producers present will think they are looking for work; if they stay very late they will be considered partygoers and perhaps lushes, irresponsible in their work."

That was good advice. The "soap" actress was telling me to go to Hollywood and work, to use whatever talent I had, but to realize that stardom was often fleeting, like a meteor. I had no training to be an actress and she was telling me that quick stardom wouldn't be that simple. She admonished me not to take myself too seriously if suddenly I got good parts with salary to match.

Fortunately—although I didn't see it that way at the time—I didn't realize immediate stardom. In a way I was fearful of going to Hollywood. I had no stage experience and certainly no experience in front of a camera. I was already twenty-eight years old with only radio, dance bands and club appearances behind me. But I certainly thirsted for the spotlight, like so many others who have come to Tinseltown with stars in their eyes.

In those days I took my son Tom to church because I wanted spiritual security for him. Ironically, he already knew the Lord personally; I was the one who needed Him! As I listened to messages preached about Jesus Christ, my heart pounded with conviction. I knew I should follow His star but I was afraid. For a long time I did not personally ask Him into the tabernacle of my heart. And I paid serious consequences. What little success I did have in the film business or in any part of my career never seemed to be enough. I had an empty space inside that stardom could not fill. Jesus, the real Star, was the only One Who could.

"Celebrity" Wasn't Used Forty Years Ago

When I was trying to break into films during the 1940s, I wasn't even aware of any term like "celebrityism." Author Richard Schickel is right when he says that forty years ago the word *celebrity* was not used in print or conversation. In his book, *Intimate Strangers: The Culture of Celebrity*, Schickel says that most of the people you read or heard about were successful or famous because they "paid their dues." That is, they progressed logically in their achievements. First they sought to do well in their chosen craft or profession. Then they might become famous, but it was not their primary goal. High achievers handled fame carefully, regulating it, ". . . so that it did not become a nuisance, or worse, actually begin to distort one's personality, interfere with the discharge of one's duties, or render one tiresome to others."[1]

Mainly through the medium of television, the term *celebrity* came into vogue a decade or two ago. Now people could become famous overnight. They could get exposure to millions without having to work that hard to become proficient in a craft. Today we are in the age of the instant success, the instant star, the instant celebrity. Today it is possible to gain celebrity status by doing anything from writing one book to cutting one hot-selling record to winning the lottery.

I'm not saying there wasn't idolizing of film stars and other famous people back in the 1940s. There was. But everything has escalated today. As never before, celebrityism tempts us to make idols of entertainers, or for that matter, of anyone who gains the spotlight or becomes newsworthy.

Celebrityism is a disease, not just of the mind but of the soul. We fall into its trap whenever we give anyone undue loyalty, allegiance or attention.

TV Has Changed Everything

The old Hollywood star system has changed since the advent of television. "Stars" loom more quickly on the horizon, and often fade just as quickly. For example, rock stars are catapulted into instant fame with attendant soaring salaries and unbelievable press hype. The youngsters begin to feel they are very, very important, but they can be thrown almost as quickly as an irate wild Brahma bull can throw an unwary cowboy.

Several years ago a popular musical group claimed, "We are more popular than Jesus Christ." Today their popularity has waned, but the Star of Jesus shines more brightly than ever.

Celebrityism means losing your perspective about someone who has talent and gifts you appreciate. Instead of simply enjoying them, having affection for them and being grateful for their gifts, it's just a short step over the line to worshiping them. When that happens you have another god that you put before God Himself, and God has always taken a dim view of that! (See Exodus 20:3.)

A term in common use while I was growing up was "matinee idol"—a label referring to movie stars who thrilled thousands at the cinema on Saturday afternoons. When I headed for Hollywood, I too dreamed of being a matinee idol—until Christ came in and woke me up.

We often say that stars and other celebrities are "larger than life." This cliché has an ominous meaning: When a celebrity becomes larger than life, he or she blocks out the sun, which can also be spelled S-O-N. Celebrityism is pulling people away from the One they should be worshiping—Jesus Christ.

The Church Has Its Own Star System

I am not talking only about people who have no interest in the Lord or spiritual concerns. My biggest concern is the church itself, where we have our own star system going full blast. In his excellent book, *Whatever Happened to Ordinary Christians?*, Jim Smoke rips away the mask of hypocrisy worn in many churches:

> Christian "stars" are people who have been elevated above the ordinary by their extraordinary accomplishments. We tend to rate Christian personalities like restaurants. The top ones get a five-star rating (they're invited to the biggest and best Christian confabs). Four stars receive second-level invitations (with the chance to appear in megachurches). The three stars get to debut at denominational conclaves. The two stars appear in churches with less than 500 members. The one stars are spending their time polishing their newly acquired stars and wondering how to fill their calendars.
>
> It is easy to spend our time star gazing, star worshipping, star shopping and star following. It is also becoming very easy to let the extraordinary Christian stars do the ministry that all ordinary Christians are called by Christ to do.[2]

Why Are We Such Star Gazers?

There are many explanations for celebrityism, but I'll leave most of those to the sociologists and talk about two things I see working in us all:

> 1. Our needs to feel that we have worth, that life has meaning, and that we can make a difference;
> 2. How these needs tempt us to put more importance on acquiring things, success and fame rather than on God.

Ironically, the way to true self-worth and a meaningful life is through faith in Christ. But somehow we can get sidetracked—actually the devil is a master at leading us astray.

One problem is that we think we're protected because we are believers. We tell ourselves we would never get sucked into anything blatantly sinful. What makes that attitude so dangerous is that it's partially true. It's easy to spot the kind of status-seeking that totally ignores God and makes self-centeredness the driving force of life.

For example, an article entitled "The New Status Seekers" appeared at the end of 1987, discussing how people in the 1980s have become more and more creative in their efforts to show others they have arrived. According to the authors of this article, status-seeking goes through certain cycles.

People have always sought status and tried not only to keep up with the Joneses but to outdo them in one way or the other. Back in the 1950s, Vance Packard wrote a best seller called *The Status Seekers* in which he coined the term "status straining." The '50s were marked by acquisition, getting all you could as fast as you could. The idea was to own something elaborate, if possible, much more elaborate than your neighbor's. This was how you achieved status. In the 1960s and '70s there was a backlash. The Volkswagen Beetle, anything but a mark of material luxury, became popular. Having status back then, particularly among the young, focused on driving one of those funny little bugs.

As people moved through the '60s and '70s they prided

themselves more on what they experienced than on what they possessed. They liked to talk about where they went out to eat or where they traveled.

And then came the '80s and we were back to acquiring things again. But this bubble burst in the fall of 1987 with the stock market crash. We have moved beyond the frantic acquisition of things, which was so typical of the early 1980s, and are heading for what some call "status burnout."

Faith Popcorn (yes, that's her real name) is chairman of a marketing firm that specializes in talking about trends—what's in, what's out, what's coming up, and so on. She calls the present phenomenon "yuppie glut" and believes the next big trend will totally reverse the chasing after material things and status. She calls it "cashing out," which means that people are turning down promotions, long hours and lots of traveling in order to spend more time with family, friends and neighbors.

Now the way to have status is through relationships and associations. People are realizing again that money simply isn't enough; they are trying to get back to basic values. According to a 1987 Roper Poll, when asked what constituted success in their eyes, Americans said: "Being a good parent, having a happy marriage, enjoying a happy relationship with another, having friends who respect them, being one of the best at their job. Measures of material affluence finished near the bottom of the list."[3]

While these changes sound positive, there is still a catch— and a very real danger. Whatever a new trend might be, if the goal is status, impressing others and being "cool" and "in," it is just more narcissism packaged a little differently. You can want a happy marriage and family and happy relationships, but if you're doing it to gain status, you are not serving God but yourself.

What Is "Best" for Believers?

Are Christians immune to status-seeking? Hardly. Status-seeking tempts believers right along with everyone else.

In church we nod agreement when the pastor quotes Jesus, Who said that anyone who wants to be great must become a servant of all (see Matt. 20:26). But if we're honest, we admit it's far more intriguing when a speaker or writer blends the gospel with promises of health, wealth and well-being. How well I remember a close friend once telling me, "Christians should go 'first cabin.'" The idea was that as God's children we should show the world that our Heavenly Father owns everything anyway and just as an earthly father wants the best for his child, God wants His children to have the best too.

The problem with that thinking is that it's easy to get confused about what the "best" really is. The Bible is very clear that the best in life is not comprised of material things but of spiritual development.

Theologian J. I. Packer is right when he says our society has moved far from what the Bible teaches and has instead developed a kind of "hot tub religion," a philosophy emphasizing egocentricity and making happiness our highest goal. Our "hot tub" approach to Christianity tempts us to decline Jesus' invitation to deny ourselves and to reject God's disciplinary program for spiritual growth. It's much more attractive to talk about being "content" and "fulfilled."[4]

Once while Jesus was preaching, a scribe (teacher of the law) said, "I will follow You wherever you go." But Jesus simply replied, "Foxes have holes and birds of the air have nests, but the Son of Man has no place to lay his head" (Matt. 8:20). What Jesus was telling the scribe was to count the cost, to realize that if he wanted to follow Christ, he had to give up the emphasis on things and certainly the priority of status.

Nothing gets old faster than a new thing and nothing can vanish more quickly than status in the eyes of those who are always looking to see who has what, who's done the most, who is really "in" and beautiful this month.

Jesus knew we would face all this in the twentieth century, even as He said, "Do not store up for yourselves treasures on earth, where moth and rust destroy, and where thieves break in and steal. But store up for yourselves treasures in heaven, where moth and rust do not destroy, and where thieves do not break in and steal. For where your treasure is, there your heart will be also" (Matt. 6:19–21).

In the same sermon, Jesus also said we can't serve two

masters because we will wind up hating one and loving the other: "You cannot serve both God and Money" (Matt. 6:24).

There are many interpretations of what Jesus meant in these passages, especially when it comes to hiring pastors or other people for ministry. Some churches take terrible advantage of a pastor or a guest speaker and pay little or nothing, citing passages like these in the sixth chapter of Matthew to justify their miserliness. Some of them even like to say, "Money is the root of all evil," which is a misquote of what Paul actually wrote to Timothy: "The *love* of money is the root of all evil." He also said some people let the lust for money lure them from the faith and they can come to all kinds of grief (see 1 Tim. 6:10).

I think Paul is pinpointing the issue when he says the love of money is the problem. Do we love money or God? As Jesus said, we can't really do justice to loving both. Only one can take first place. Jesus told us not to worry about things like what we would eat or drink or wear: "For the pagans run after all these things, and your heavenly Father knows that you need them. But seek first his kingdom and his righteousness, and all these things will be given to you as well" (Matt. 6:32–33).

God Meets Needs, Not Greeds

Jesus' words are for all status seekers—in the first century or the twentieth. When we become preoccupied with eating and drinking graciously and lavishly, when we start emphasizing what we wear to be sure we're always in style, when we start believing the lies of commercials that tell us "You *are* what you drive," we have crossed the line and love money more than God.

As usual, it's a question of balance. As someone said, "God will provide for our needs, not our greeds." It's so very easy to get greed mixed with what we really need.

Jesus also said, "The laborer is worthy of his hire" (Luke 10:7, KJV). I believe He meant that the laborer is worthy of having his needs met so he can serve adequately and well. I don't subscribe to the oft-prevailing notion that ministers should drive second-hand cars with over 100,000 miles on them, or that they, their wives or their children should wear only hand-me-down clothes. I also believe that those who travel on speaking circuits in ministry should have their expenses met and be remunerated adequately but not exorbitantly for their time.

I still do a lot of traveling for ministry and cover thousands of miles per year. I try to be careful not to confuse my needs with my greeds. Now that I'm in my mid-seventies, I do believe that the rigors of travel dictate my use of a first-class seat. Not because I want to feel important or have status. It's simply a matter of traveling comfortably so I can arrive as rested as possible. In addition, there is usually less confusion and noise, giving me the chance to be quiet, meditate, pray and even do some writing.

When I arrive at my destination, I often raise eyebrows because I'm traveling alone. "Where's your secretary?" people want to know. I always travel alone and I always travel light. That's another reason why I use a first-class seat. I carry everything I have on board and use one of those little collapsible dollies to wheel my own luggage around in an airport.

I've had people ask me, "Where are all your trunks?" They seem to think I should have eight or ten pieces of baggage. And I simply say, "For what? I don't have time for that. Besides, I don't *need* all that."

I don't require a limousine to pick me up on arrival and I don't covet posh hotel suites. Sometimes I protest about my accommodations to the pastor or the person coordinating my appearance. He usually explains that the hotel donated the suite free of charge, but a comfortable hotel room is all I need.

I don't ever want things or status to possess me. But neither am I interested in plaiting laurels for my head and playing the role of the "humble, unassuming Christian." What I really want is what is spiritually good for me. It all comes back to needs, not greeds. It's so easy to get a rather rosy view of what God wants for His children!

Should Speakers Charge a Fee?

There is much difference of opinion concerning speaker fees. I have been asked why I charge a fee when Jesus and His apostles did not. Well, neither did they have families and the expenses of maintaining a home, not to mention supporting their local church, plus missionaries, as Roy and I do.

While I was still working in motion pictures and had that income, I didn't charge anything for speaking appearances. But over the years I was gently eased out of secular work and couldn't get on a lot of programs because I was known as "a religious type." Today, speaking fees are my livelihood. Yes, obviously Roy and I have plenty of money. I wouldn't starve if I didn't get anything. But I still come back to what Jesus said, "The laborer is worthy of her wages."

I charge what I believe is a reasonable fee and then take the responsibility of being a good steward of that money. I tithe to my church and support various mission projects. Beyond that I give much more to Christian causes and charities, many times with no tax deductions, not to gain status in my own eyes or anyone else's, but simply because I *want to*.

Still, many people don't understand. They don't realize there is a tremendous investment in travel, equipment, clothes and personal appearance. The costs are astronomical, but so are people's expectations. Maybe Paul or Peter could show up dusty or grubby and be welcomed with open arms, but in this culture you're expected to look as if you're right out of the bandbox. And if you don't, you can't be very effective.

I'm aware that what I'm saying here could easily be misunderstood as rationalizing or justifying myself. Or some might say, "She's trying to impress us with how spiritual she is." I'll have to take that risk because I want to share my own heart with you and let you know where I stand. In any book on "curing celebrityism," these things must be addressed. I wrestle with these questions all the time and I'm certainly not in it for the money, per se. I'm always ready and open for God's further guidance. I travel and speak, not for my benefit, but for His. I have tried to lower my fees, but my agents tell me, "If your fee is too low, we can't handle you."

Three Things That Are Undoing Us

Every now and then I'm tempted to quit ministering and traveling and just stay at home and work in my own church. But just about the time I start to weaken, I get a letter or a comment from a stranger and hear that one of my books, or something I've said on television, or at a concert, led someone to Christ. And every once in a while I hear that something I've said kept someone from suicide.

And that keeps me going into the thick of battle. I always go back to what Paul said in Ephesians 6:12: "For our struggle is not against flesh and blood, but against the rulers, against the authorities, against the powers of this dark world and against the spiritual forces of evil in the heavenly realms."

Paul had no idea how appropriate his words would be for the twentieth century. Take a look around you. Money, power and sex are undoing us. Richard Foster is right: "The crying need today is for people to live faithfully."[5] Never are these words more true than in regard to the three issues Foster writes about in his fine book, *Money, Sex, and Power*. As he says, nothing touches us ". . . more profoundly or more universally. No themes are more inseparably intertwined. No topics cause more controversy. No human realities have greater power to bless or to curse. No three things have been more sought after or more in need of a Christian response."[6]

For all of us, women and men, there is a fine line between looking as nice as possible to glorify our Creator and going overboard with jewelry, clothes, makeup, etc. Because of my show business background, I have to examine myself constantly on this very issue. It's true that I have often been guilty of being too preoccupied with my wardrobe. In one of my earlier books, I wrote about the time I finished speaking to a crowd of two thousand women and, feeling elated, went back to my hotel room to flip on TV and relax for a few minutes.

A young comedian on a talk show was telling about the time a boisterous woman almost ruined his act with her remarks. Apparently she had had far too much to drink and he couldn't quiet her.

As his story unfolded, the comedian said, "I walked over to her table to confront her and this gal was dressed as if she were going to meet Dale Evans."

I sat bolt upright in bed, wondering, "What did he mean *by that?*" The comedian went on telling the talk show host his story. He asked the woman what she did for a living and without hesitation she said she was a hooker. At this the studio audience roared with a kind of raucous laughter common on this particular "late-late" show. My first reaction was "What an insult!" But in a few minutes I started to laugh. Perhaps this was the Lord's way of taking me down a few pegs for being too concerned about wardrobe. I thanked Him for grace to laugh at myself and asked for the grace to be less vain in the future.[7]

What Is My True Love?

The comedian's crack about being "dressed fit to go visit Dale Evans" was his opinion, of course. Some people might agree with him, but to others my clothes might not look that extravagant at all. Again, we come back to that question of balance. Where is my heart? What is my true love? Jesus said we can't serve God and money. Paul warned us that the love of money plants evil in our hearts. The love of money will have us excluding time spent in the Bible and in prayer. The love of money will preoccupy us and lure us into the trap of trying to please the world with how we look and act, where we go, and what we drive.

I'm not interested in driving a Mercedes, BMW, or any other prestige car. All I care about is having something that can get me to the airport and back with no engine trouble. And, the opinions of the comedian notwithstanding, I don't wear designer clothes. They're just not important to me. What is important is looking as nice as I can for the Lord when I go out.

I do all my own housework, except having a woman come in once a week to do the heavy cleaning. Today I have six children, sixteen grandchildren and fifteen great-grandchildren—and I've never been so busy in my whole life. In my mid-seventies, I'm busier than I was in my thirties! It's the Lord Who keeps me going and all I want is to be available to Him. I just want to stay young at heart and open to His will. I love Jesus' words, "Blessed are the meek" (Matt. 5:5). To be meek means to be teachable, and that's what I want to be.

In chapter two of the First Epistle of John, the apostle writes about "overcoming the evil one" (see vv. 12-14). Then he goes on to teach Christians how to do that: "Do not love the world or anything in the world. If anyone loves the world, the love of the Father is not in him. For everything in the world—the cravings of sinful man, the lust of his eyes and the boasting of what he has and does—comes not from the Father but from the world" (1 John 2:15-16).

When the apostle John wrote those words he was a very old man—some say nearly a hundred, possibly older. He was the last living person who had ever seen and touched Jesus Christ. He had seen it all and knew exactly what he was talking about. Satan attacks through our desires, through our fantasy life, and through our insatiable need to stand out and have status—to boast about what we have and what we've done.

Because Satan despises the Lord Jesus Christ and His redemptive work, he will go to any length to attack it. But he works subtly, quietly and often appears as an angel of light.

Scandals Can Be a Blessing

In one sense the shocking televangelists' scandals of 1987-1988 are a blessing because they have made us keenly aware of how vulnerable we all are. I know all this has made me look deeply into my own heart. As the psalmist said, "Search me, O God, and know my heart; test me and know my anxious thoughts. See if there is any offensive way in me, and lead me in the way everlasting" (Ps. 139:23-24).

Scandals are easy to sensationalize. The secular press has had a field day with Christian bashing, and if Christians aren't careful they will bash their own wounded ones as well.

It's easy to point the finger and shake the head and criticize. But celebrityism is a pervasive force that affects all of us. We are all involved and we all must examine ourselves. Is Jesus the only Star in our lives, or are there others?

When I sing at a Christian concert or speak at some Christian function, very often I cringe at flowery introductions that list credits, tributes and accolades. I always get up and comment that, while I appreciate the kind words, I want to declare, "There is only one Star here tonight!"

These words come to you straight from my heart. The longer I continue my Christian pilgrimage, the more I desire to decrease personally and to have Jesus increase in the hearts of people I touch.

I covet your prayers. I really do, because it's just too easy for those in the spotlight to be drawn away by their own desires and be enticed (see James 1:13–15). In the next two chapters we'll look at how and why this can happen, even to those whom we love and admire, and what we can learn from their mistakes.

4

The Heritage of
Celebrityism

During the past year I have often been asked, "Dale, what do you think about the scandals involving the Bakkers and Jimmy Swaggart?"

I usually respond by saying that Satan is a very wily fellow and always attacks the church at its most vulnerable spot. For many years I have seen the subtle danger in our "Christian celebrity system." In a book I wrote in 1980, I talked about the Christian "star complex." If we are not thoroughly committed to Jesus and willing to let His Spirit guide, it is all too easy to get carried away in the flesh and perform instead of minister.

Many years in the entertainment business have shown me how treacherous the ego can be, particularly if a large crowd is involved. But anyone who tries to minister in the name of Christ must remember it's not the gospel according to Pat Boone, Norma Zimmer, Nicky Cruz, Chuck Colson, Johnny Cash, Evie, Jim Bakker, Jimmy Swaggart or Roy and Dale Rogers that gets the job done. *Always* it has to be the gospel according to Jesus Christ.

In 1980 I wrote, "Even the most committed Christians are prone to fall short of the glory of God. We are still human. Please, please do not be a 'Christian-celebrity-watcher' but a Christ watcher! . . . . as a Christian witness, I pray the Lord will jerk the leash on me if I run ahead in the flesh. Believe me, it is easy to do."[1]

I meant every word I wrote then and today those words take on even more significance. If any group should be aware of the foolishness and disobedience in a system of celebrities or stars, it should be the body of Christ. Today's so-called "stars" are no more than meteors—not even a brief flicker of a match compared to the light of eternity. Jesus is the only Star, now and forever.

Think of the bright stars of yesteryear, some quite luminous in their time, who are no longer remembered. Others are still remembered by aging fans who travel to worship at their graves and who continue to buy their recordings or photographs. But the masses forget as generations come and go. Only Jesus remains a steadfast light now and forever.

Devoted Fans Immortalized Elvis

Perhaps no star has been immortalized by devoted fans more than Elvis Presley. During his lifetime his record sales hit five hundred million, and another eight million were sold in the five days following his death on August 16, 1977. Up to a million persons visit his grave at the Graceland Mansion every year. Many reverently lay flowers on the gravestone while others take away twigs or blades of grass—anything they can find as a keepsake.

Presley fans purchase souvenirs all over Memphis. You can buy anything from a copy of the newspaper that recorded Elvis' death to a bogus dollar bill featuring his picture in place of George Washington's. Also for sale are copies of his driver's license and last will and testament. You can even buy one-inch square pieces of his first tombstone, which was cut up for souvenir sales and another larger one put in its place.

Go to the gravesite and you can find thousands of grief-stricken messages scrawled on the wall. For example:

"The king is dead. Long live the king."

"You can lose your President, but [Elvis] is like a god, and if you lose your god, you go crazy."

"A modern, true living messiah."[2]

The word *messiah* fits the image many of Elvis' fans have of their idol. At a special gathering in Presley's honor at Las Vegas, a photographer who had snapped more than eighty thousand photographs of Elvis Presley declared, "The last time this happened was two thousand years ago. And this time it's getting better press."[3]

Rick Stanley Grew Up at Graceland

Not long ago I had the pleasure of breakfasting with the evangelist Rick Stanley while in Birmingham, Alabama, for a starlight crusade, where we both were guests. In his book, *The Touch of Two Kings,* Rick writes about growing up as the stepbrother of Elvis Presley. He lived with Elvis at his home in Graceland in Memphis, Tennessee, and worshiped him as his star, to the point of almost destroying his life with drugs and alcohol.

When Rick was five years old, his mother divorced his father and married Vernon Presley, whose son, Elvis, had already established himself as the outstanding star of early rock and roll. Rick, his older brother, Billy, and younger brother, David, were then whisked to the Graceland Mansion into a world of wealth and opulence that left them stunned. When they drove up to the mansion, there were cars everywhere, all of them belonging to Elvis.

When they walked upstairs to meet Elvis, they found him sitting by his record player listening to gospel music—which was his habit. When he saw Rick and his brothers, he scooped all three of them up in his arms and then said to his father, "These are MY little brothers, now, Dad, and that's just the way I'm going to treat them."[4]

Elvis was twenty-five at the time and his star was rising faster than an Atlas rocket. He had already hit the top of the pop charts, appeared on the Ed Sullivan Show, made movies and done a highly publicized stint in the Army. Roy and I were on that same show with Elvis, and I can still remember Ed Sullivan refusing to allow Presley to be photographed from the waist down when he did his act.

The morning after Rick and his brothers arrived at Graceland, they got a taste of Elvis' success and generosity. They were greeted with three bicycles, three tricycles, three scooters, three little tanks, three machine guns—three of every toy they could think of. There was also a large swing set that had been installed in the backyard during the night.

Rick settled into a fairy tale life, which included being driven to his first grade classes at school by Elberta the maid in Elvis' pink Cadillac.

"Wonder Times" Lasted All Night

The barrage of toys was only the beginning. As Rick grew up, he experienced what he called "wonder times" with Elvis. Sometimes Elvis rented an entire amusement park for his friends and his little brothers. They could ride whatever they wanted, as often as they liked, all night long. Not only did Elvis rent the park, but all the workers as well. And he paid them bonuses for taking good care of everyone.

Or sometimes Elvis rented a movie theatre from midnight until dawn. Rick remembers watching movies literally all through the night, and of course, all the concessions were free—candy bars, Cokes, popcorn—as much as he could consume.

Rick's mother tried to keep a tight rein on him, but it was useless. Elvis charmed her into letting him spoil Rick and his brothers and, as soon as he was out of her sight, Rick learned about life's temptations firsthand. In eighth grade, a friend introduced Rick to alcohol and he became desperately sick from drinking huge glasses of hard liquor to prove he was "cool." In tenth grade, one of the school football stars introduced him to pot.

By age sixteen, Rick was invited by Elvis to become his personal aide, a member of a tight-knit group of eight to ten young men known as the "Memphis Mafia." The Memphis Mafia kept Elvis' tours running smoothly and devoted their lives to meeting his personal needs. Their written code of ethics demanded total loyalty to "the King." Rick remembers the slogan of their air-tight group—"'Take care of business,' of 'TCB' with a lightning bolt emblazoned across it. It was on all of our jackets, on some of the cars, and on the tail of the jet. 'TCB'—slash, slash, slash. TAKE CARE OF BUSINESS."[5]

Rick made his first trip with Elvis and the rest of the Memphis Mafia when the group flew on the rock star's personal jet to Washington, D.C., to see President Nixon. They weren't particularly invited, but Elvis thought it would be a good idea.

It was on that trip that Rick learned about the double standard that Elvis lived by. As they stepped off the plane, the girl chosen for Elvis was waiting, and there were women waiting for other men in the group, most of whom were also married. Elvis warned Rick never to discuss what he saw. This was "just the way it is." According to Rick, Elvis Presley was a bundle of contradictions. He loved playing gospel music in his home, but adultery was a constant part of his lifestyle. Elvis hitched his wagon to the star of public acclaim at any cost and in the end it cost him his life.

The Bible says, "Jesus is the light of the world," but Elvis twisted his body and sang his heart out in the glare of earthly spotlights, often feeling dark and desperate inside. There was a constant gnawing that could not be satisfied with what the world had to offer.

On stage Elvis lost himself in his music as he tried to please an ever-demanding public and, finally, he broke from outer exhaustion and inner chaos. Elvis Presley was a generous, giving person but his incredible generosity failed to satisfy his deep inner hunger. He was a true star of stars who shone with astounding intensity, but his brightness suddenly disappeared into a cold grave in Memphis.

At the End, Elvis Just Didn't Care

Near the end of Elvis' life his wife, Priscilla, filed for divorce. She could no longer take his adulterous escapades. According to Rick Stanley, ". . . he had different women in most places he went. He might do a show in Vegas for thirty days and not allow his wife to come out during that time. She couldn't even come while he was making films. He would sometimes go to Palm

Springs on the weekends, and there would be other women. This was the cold truth."[6]

When Elvis finally lost Priscilla to another man (a karate instructor), his ego was bruised and he took the loss very hard. He started to neglect his appearance, began to overeat and didn't care about anything. He refused performances and turned down interviews. In Rick's words, "He flat made a nose dive."

Rick "nose dived" as well and was turning his brain to mush with drugs of all kinds. He began shooting up at age eighteen when he did his first "rig" (needle) at a friend's apartment in Memphis. After that, he was a frequent heroin user.

The pace Elvis kept was incredible. In *The Touch of Two Kings* Rick wrote, "I knew he couldn't keep going. Sooner or later he would snap. These were the last days when Elvis was heading downward like a coming storm. His body was a time bomb— ravished from chemicals, stimuli and exhaustion."[7]

Day after day Elvis did his show and then went to bed immediately. Gone were the times when his inner circle gathered with him after a show and visited for hours. Now he looked tortured and tired. And the only thing that seemed to bring him any joy at all was his little daughter, Lisa Marie.

The crowning blow came when several of Elvis' Memphis Mafia aides decided to do an exposé of his life entitled *Elvis: What Happened?* (by Steve Dunleavy, published in 1982 by Ballantine). Somehow Elvis obtained an outline of the book and was crushed when he saw what his "friends" were going to say. Rick had no part in this book and calls it "unfair, slanted, and a personal vendetta . . . ."

But just knowing about the book broke Elvis' spirit even further. Rick believes he lost his desire to live from that time on. The night before Elvis died, Rick was on the phone with Robyn, the girl who had been witnessing to him for years. He remembers her saying, "What's it going to take, Rick? What's it going to take for you to come to Christ?"

After the phone call, Rick went upstairs to see why Elvis had sent for him. The rock and roll king was in the middle of his big bed with books, including the Bible, scattered everywhere.

Rick saw the Bible and told Elvis about his friend Robyn and what she had been sharing with him about Christ. The two of them talked earnestly and Rick remembers what Elvis said: "Rick, she's right. You know that, don't you?"

All Rick could manage was, "Yeah, I guess so." Elvis looked very tired and bewildered, devastated over the book his former friends were writing about him. At one point he bowed his head and said, "Lord, show me the way." Then he looked up and said something that Rick Stanley will remember to his dying day: "Rick, we should all begin to live for Christ."

The next morning Elvis Presley was found dead in his bathroom by Rick's younger brother, David, and his father, Vernon.[8]

As I talked with Rick Stanley, he told me he believes Elvis Presley knew Christ personally. He simply "had hold of a tiger's tail" and couldn't let go. Who knows what Elvis could have accomplished for many more years had he followed the enduring Star of Hope instead of the star of wealth, fame and celebrity that always fades in the end?

After his stepbrother's death, Rick Stanley plunged even more deeply into drugs and despair. But later he was saved physically and mentally, as well as spiritually, mainly through the efforts of his friend, Robyn, who today is his wife.

After coming to Christ, Rick attended Criswell Bible Institute and graduated from Southwestern Baptist Theological Seminary in 1986. For the last several years, he has spoken in approximately one thousand revivals and conferences in churches across America and Europe. He has also spoken in more than two hundred high schools each year concerning problems related to drugs and alcohol. Rick is a powerful witness for Christ and stands unwaveringly against the kind of lifestyle he had as a member of Elvis' Memphis Mafia. He is all too familiar with what too much money, fame and celebrity can do.

The PTL Flap Shook Us All

I pray that Rick Stanley can keep his perspective and not get sucked into the kind of whirlpool that engulfed Jim and Tammy

Faye Bakker, as well as Jimmy Swaggart. The PTL flap gave the secular press a field day throughout most of 1987. That scandal had barely died down when Jimmy Swaggart's problems came to light in February 1988, almost a year after Bakker's affair with Jessica Hahn had been revealed.

To his credit, Jim Bakker didn't gloat over Swaggart's shame and embarrassment. News reports quoted him as saying he had forgiven Swaggart long ago for denouncing his adultery with Jessica Hahn and comparing him to a cancer that needed to be excised from the body of Christ.

"We are living in forgiveness," said Jim Bakker. "I choose to forgive those who have opposed us."[9]

In that same news story, Bakker advised Swaggart not to make any decisions for thirty days. Of his own resignation from his huge television ministry, Bakker said, "They gave me only a few hours. If I had had thirty days I would not have given up PTL. You can't make a decision under pressure."

When approached in his car by TV mini-cams, Bakker commented on Swaggart saying, "Only those without sin can throw stones."

I agree. Jesus said, "Do not judge, or you too will be judged" (see Matt. 7:1). I prefer not to throw stones at Jim Bakker or Jimmy Swaggart but to learn from their mistakes instead. None of us has the right to bend to pick up a single pebble. Nonetheless, as Christians grapple with their own temptations and sins, they can't help but feel a bit puzzled when men who have gladly accepted the role of spiritual leader to literally millions of people drop boulders on their own heads. I am afraid they simply got their eyes on the empires they were building instead of keeping their eyes on the Star and walking in His light.

Can these fallen men be forgiven? Of course. I believe with all my heart that the grace of God is based on His unlimited forgiveness and mercy. Jesus taught us to forgive seventy times seven —that is, indefinitely, again and again (see Matt. 18:21-22). But God's grace is never so open-minded that justice falls through the cracks. The lesson in the fall of celebrity televangelists is not to gather our self-righteous skirts and shun or deride them, but to see that the terrible power of God's grace also includes something called justice.

The Lord's love and mercy reach far beyond what we can ask or think. There is only one Star. We can try to shine brighter than He does; we can try to block Him out or ignore Him. Worst of all, we can give Him lip service from careless, confused or even empty hearts (see 2 Tim. 3:5). The mind-boggling truth of Scripture is that God's grace gives us freedom to make all these terrible mistakes and more, and yet His love remains as strong as ever. He cannot deny Himself (2 Tim. 2:13). Nothing can separate us from the burning bright love of the One Who is the only Star (see Rom. 8:38). His brightness always shines into the deepest recesses of our hearts and exposes our true thoughts and intents (see Heb. 4:12).

An old cliché says "misery loves company." It is even more true that hypocrisy is very lonely and has its own reward.

I appeared on PTL several times—in fact, I had been on the show just a week before the story of Jim Bakker's adulterous affair with Jessica Hahn was exposed. If Jim is half the disciple I believed he was when I appeared on PTL programs, he will realize that he was living in hypocrisy. No Christian who is walking with the Lord pays hush money to anyone. After studying the evidence, executives of the Assemblies of God released a statement saying, "The evidence seems to indicate that effort and money have been expended to cover moral failure."[10]

Like everyone else, I don't know how much of the reports about the Bakkers' private lives is true. I do know that if you go to a party and play the game "Whisper," the original story can change into something completely different by the time it is repeated all the way around the room.

As serious as the sexual scandal sounds, it was only the tip of the iceberg regarding PTL's problems. As host of PTL, Jim Bakker had tremendous power. He built a television empire with donations from his viewers who gave something like $132 million a year to keep the entire ministry going. When you are bringing in that kind of money and reaching millions of people, it's easy to lose your perspective. Lord Acton once warned: "Power corrupts and absolute power corrupts absolutely."

In the aftermath of his resignation, Jim Bakker faced lawsuits seeking the return of millions of dollars he had allegedly squandered or misused while leading PTL and the Heritage U.S.A. Theme Park he and Tammy Faye developed in Charlotte, North Carolina.

When Bakker resigned, he asked Jerry Falwell to take charge of the PTL ministry. Next he accused Jimmy Swaggart of a "hostile takeover," apparently because he believed Swaggart to be the one who had reported Bakker's sexual indiscretions to the National Council of the Assemblies of God, of which Bakker and Swaggart were members. In a short time, however, Bakker had broken fellowship with Falwell, particularly when the new leader tried to clear up the financial mess at PTL. A new PTL board halted all payments to the Bakkers, a sum which had totaled $1.6 million in 1986 in salary and bonuses and $640,000 during the first three months of 1987.

In November 1987, PTL filed bankruptcy for protection from creditors who were owed $60 million. In turn, PTL sued the Bakkers and other former PTL leaders for $52 million, charging mismanagement and "personal enrichment."[11]

In December 1987, the Internal Revenue Service filed reports in U.S. Bankruptcy Court concerning excessive compensation to the Bakkers and other PTL officials that they claimed totaled $14.86 million between 1981 and 1987. Of that amount, $9.36 million supposedly went to the Bakkers, according to I.R.S. charges.[12]

On April 22, 1988, the IRS revoked PTL's tax-exempt status, claiming PTL owes over $50 million in back taxes from June 1983 to June 1987. An IRS spokesman stated that PTL had not operated within the guidelines of its original charter and that it had excessive, unrelated business income or income not in keeping with tax exempt purposes.[13]

Sorting out the financial tangle may take years. In the meantime, Jim and Tammy Faye must sort out their lives. In the fall of 1987, the Bakkers moved from Palm Springs, California, where they had stayed since the scandal broke in March, and took up residence in Gatlinburg, Tennessee, where Bakker planned to think through his problems and write his autobiography. But early

in 1988 new stories had them turning up again in Palm Springs
with lavish plans for building a desert complex that would include
a hotel, golf course and religious theme park to rival Heritage
U.S.A. in North Carolina.[14]

In addition to seeking support for their new complex—to
be called Heritage Springs International—the Bakkers hoped to
revive their Jim and Tammy TV show. In addition to Jim's autobiography, an NBC movie of the week, "Fall from Grace," was also
reported to be in the works.*

In an article appearing in the *Los Angeles Times*, Bakker was
quoted: "If I can't get back up, then this gospel is not true. If I
can't be forgiven of anything and go on, and if I can't be restored,
then this Bible doesn't work."[15]

In one sense, Jim Bakker is absolutely right. Any of us who
claim Christ as Savior can be forgiven and restored. That's the
clear promise of 1 John 1:9: "If we confess our sins, he is faithful
and just and will forgive us our sins and purify us from all
unrighteousness."

---

* The Bakker story continued as this book was being prepared for publication.
According to news reports during June 1988, the Bakkers had moved to the Fort Mill,
South Carolina area, just a few minutes from Heritage U.S.A., and were pursuing as many
as four different plans to buy or rent the PTL ministry, using a $100 million line of credit
provided by an unnamed lender. M. C. Bennett, newly appointed by the court as PTL
trustee, said that, if substantiated, "Bakker's offer would be considered along with at least
three others, one of which was for $200 million."

Bakker's attorney said that one plan called for Bakker's rental of the Heritage
Grand Hotel and adjacent water park and purchase of air time on the PTL television
network. Bennett was reported as saying that putting the Bakkers back on the air would
be ". . . extremely difficult until their name is cleared." As of July 1988, the Bakkers
faced: (1) a Federal grand jury investigation of their fiscal management while at PTL; (2) a
$52 million lawsuit by PTL, filed by former PTL trustee, David Clark, against the Bakkers
for "gross and willful mismanagement"; (3) a $167 million claim filed on behalf of 114,000
Lifetime Partners, who made $1,000 contributions to PTL in exchange for three nights
and four days' free use of Heritage U.S.A. facilities yearly for the rest of their lives.

At the time M. C. Bennett was appointed PTL trustee, the ministry faced
bankruptcy with debts estimated at $130 million and the loss of nearly 25 percent of its TV
stations. Bennett's goal was to develop a new reorganization plan to sell Heritage U.S.A.,
and establish a debt-free, nonprofit ministry. (See "Bakker Competes to Buy Back PTL,"
Associated Press Release, *Los Angeles Herald Examiner*, 30 June 1988, p. A-6; also see Eric
Levin with Gail Cameron Wescott, "It's Jim & Tammy Time Again!" *People Weekly*, 4 July
1988, pp. 32–35.)

The Bible does work, but on whose timetable? Late in 1987, Kenneth Kantzer, senior editor of *Christianity Today*, wrote:

"When PTL host, Jim Bakker, betrayed the trust of his supporters by immoral conduct and extravagant living, he claimed that he had repented and that he should be restored immediately to his former role. God had forgiven him, he declared. How could Christian people do less? Some of his former followers have, indeed, forgiven him, but few observers are convinced that he should be restored to leadership."[16]

What Jim and Tammy Faye Bakker must realize is that it is not a question of being forgiven; the real issue is seeking God's will and His timing. When he headed PTL, Jim Bakker had practically unlimited power. He was accountable to nobody and I think it all got out of hand. Perhaps his ego pushed him. I recall asking a friend of mine back at Heritage U.S.A. to tell Jim to quit talking on the air about building so much and start ministering more. But I got word back that Jim had said, "God has told me to build."

Even if Jim Bakker had avoided sexual immorality, what happened was almost inevitable. Although he touched many lives for Christ, he fell into the trap of doing things in the Lord's Name but bringing glory to himself. And God will not share His glory with anyone (see Isa. 42:8).

These are hard words to write, but they need to be said, not only to the Bakkers but to us all. In the words of Cal Thomas, syndicated columnist who formerly was communications vice-president for Jerry Falwell, "Housecleaning and repentance are in order throughout evangelicalism." Thomas believes the Bakker scandal is symptomatic of a larger defect in the Christian community that has gone unchecked far too long. He said: "The church has a serious public image problem. It is the cross that ought to be the offense and not our methods. This persecution is coming because we deserve it. It's not because of our righteousness."[17]

These strong words are reminders that all of us can learn something from the Bakker and Swaggart tragedies. We will look at those lessons in the next chapter.

5

What We Can Learn from Fallen Stars

One of many jokes that made the rounds during the televangelist scandals describes two TV preachers who were discussing how they decided on the amount of offering money they would keep for themselves each week.

"My method is simple," said one. "I collect the money all week long and put it in a cardboard box. On Friday, I go into my office where I have a line drawn on the floor. I throw the box of money in the air and whatever lands to the left of the line is mine and whatever lands on the right is the Lord's."

"Well, my method is similar," replied the other. "I also collect the money in a cardboard box and at the end of the week I take it into my office. I toss it in the air and whatever the Lord catches, He can keep!"

There are several ways to react to a joke like this: (1) Chuckle loudly and believe "all televangelists are hypocrites"; (2) Smile wryly at the truth it pinpoints; (3) Become indignant over the sacrilege of poking fun at Christianity.

My initial reactions were along the lines of choices (2) and (3), but upon reflection I had a further reaction—of sadness mixed with embarrassment. In 1 Corinthians 12, the apostle Paul taught us to have no division in His body, but instead to be equally concerned for one another. "If one part suffers," wrote

Paul, "every part suffers with it; if one part is honored, every part rejoices with it" (1 Cor. 12:26).

Paul did not add, "If one part suffers dishonor, the whole body suffers dishonor also." But that is the case more often than not.

In an editorial appearing in *Christianity Today*, Executive Editor Terry Muck spoke for many Christians when he said that we are not only saddened but also embarrassed by the PTL scandal because the Bakkers are part of our family—the body of Christ.

"When one of us falls," said Muck, "we all feel the impact. Everytime it happens we vow to forgive and forget. But increasingly, our willingness is exploited; the apologies and explanation of high-profile family members have that hollow sound of a poorly written script."[1]

The Mistakes of a Few Harm All

There is no denying that the moral mistakes made by Jim Bakker, as well as Jimmy Swaggart, have dealt a severe blow to the cause of Christ. While the secular media have a field day, the world laughs and asks, "How can you Christians claim you have the answer to our problems when your own leaders fail so miserably? Where is all that power to change lives you keep talking about?"

Like it or not, we are all tarred with the same brush used on Bakker and Swaggart, even though many people would be quick to point out they never watch either man on television and support other churches and ministries that they feel are quite legitimate and aboveboard. But I don't think it's that simple. Whether you watch televangelists or not, they are a potent force in our society, and a powerful voice for the gospel of Christ. The tragedy of the mistakes made by Jim Bakker and Jimmy Swaggart is that they have brought dishonor and all kinds of difficulty to many other preachers and teachers who have ministries on radio and television.

In the fall of 1987, one poll revealed that 70 percent of the population felt that recent TV scandals would hurt Christian television evangelists. Another 30 percent felt that their trust in TV

evangelists had been eliminated. Still another 25 percent had serious reservations about how evangelists spend their money and 43
percent said that the Bakker scandal would cause them to donate
less money than they had in the past. Interestingly, 3 percent said
they would give more money than ever.

I agree with Dr. Tim LaHaye who has written in his *Capital
Report* newsletter: ". . . TV is a powerful vehicle that should be
used to reach millions for Christ. We should not judge all TV
ministries by the conduct of a few. Most are honest people sin-
cerely trying to do a faithful job for God. Of course, they should
be good stewards of that which has been entrusted to them, but
we also ought to uphold them in support and prayer."[2]

Beyond hurting others in radio and television ministry,
Bakker and Swaggart have hurt all Christians. An editorial appearing in *The Banner* in the spring of 1988 said: "The tide might
quickly turn against us. And the widely publicized fall of the
televangelists (because of sex and money—the same dark hole
through which most Americans are falling) could be the force that
pushes the pendulum the other way: people will cynically reject
not only gospel peddlers but the gospel itself."[3]

Grace Is Free, but Never Cheap

One thing we are learning from all this is that *the cost of sin is
high*; and while grace is free, it is never cheap. Unfortunately, we
live in a day when "cheap grace" is very popular. Many Christians
are tempted to emphasize the "name it and claim it" approach to
God's blessings and overlook His demands for holiness.

The apostle Paul said in effect, "Follow me as I follow
Christ" (see Phil. 3:17). In other words, if Paul's walk did not
match his talk, he was not to be followed. But the walk of Jesus
Christ matched Paul's words in every respect. At the end of his
life, imprisoned and facing execution at the hands of Caesar, Paul
could say without reservation, "I have fought the good fight, I
have finished the race, I have kept the faith. Now there is in store
for me the crown of righteousness, which the Lord, the righteous
Judge, will award to me on that day . . ." (2 Tim. 4:7-8).

Scripture says everything was created by Christ, through Christ and for Christ (see Col. 1:15–16). Through His Spirit sent at Pentecost, Christ knows how to draw our lives after Him. To follow the bright and morning Star means to lose ourselves and yield our egos to His authority. We are to walk in the light of His Spirit, Who takes charge and guides us into all truth (see John 16:13).

When his adultery with Bathsheba and coverup murder of Uriah were exposed by Nathan, David did not accuse the prophet of a "hostile takeover." Instead, he lay on the ground, fasting and weeping for several days. He confessed his sin and begged the Lord to spare the life of the child born from his adulterous union with Bathsheba. When the child died, as the Lord had decreed, David got up, washed, changed clothes, went into the house of the Lord and worshiped (see 2 Sam. 12:1–23).

When I read reports of the Bakker scandal, I was not reminded of how David acted. As Terry Muck wrote in May 1987:

> Bakker's . . . actions have raised many questions that distort our perceptions of his repentance. His initial innuendoes about a take-over come across more as excuses or, worse, attempts to divert attention from his sin. And recent attempts to portray himself as the naive victim of a worldly-wise companion further cloud the sincerity of his repentance. We need clearer affirmations that he really is sorry for what he did, and that he is willing to back that up with acts of contrition.[4]

Quo Vadis Televangelism?

Should televangelism be discontinued? Terry Muck observes that religious television isn't that much different from any other kind of TV—that is, it feeds on a star system. "Good scripts help and as far as scripts go, the gospel is the ultimate script. Yet without someone to deliver it handsomely, even the gospel gets low ratings."[5]

Muck's words are disturbing but he has a point. What he is really saying is that television and ministry are, in many ways, opposites. The strength of television ministry—the potential to reach and deeply affect millions for Christ—is also its weakness, because reaching a television audience takes charm, appeal and charisma—the qualities of a "star." Muck is right on when he says ministry is the antithesis to personality building. To minister means giving up the need to gratify ego.

Should we throw out televangelism, then, with all the dirty bath water from recent scandals? It is my guess Satan would love that—getting rid of one of the most effective of all media for spreading the gospel. The enemy of our souls is undoubtedly rubbing his hands together even now in anticipation of entrapping more Bakkers and Swaggarts to smear the name of Christ.

First Bakker, Then Swaggart

The timing of Jimmy Swaggart's confession to sexual sin seemed orchestrated by the devil himself. Just as the secular press had stopped bashing the Bakkers, Jimmy Swaggart's bombshell hit us with what seemed to be a double dose of hypocrisy. In 1987 Swaggart exposed Bakker's sexual encounter with Jessica Hahn and denounced Bakker as a "cancer on the body of Christ." In 1988 Swaggart was reported to have made visits to a red light district in New Orleans to pay prostitutes to perform pornographic acts.[6]

After he was exposed, Swaggart tearfully confessed before his huge Baton Rouge congregation and television cameras, saying he would step down from the pulpit ". . . for an undetermined, indeterminant period of time. We will leave that in the hands of the Lord."[7] To his credit, when Swaggart confessed, he called his behavior exactly what it is. In his admission of guilt before the Family Worship Center, and on television, he said: "I do not plan in any way to whitewash my sin or call it a mistake. I call it sin."[8] Swaggart charged no one with an attempted takeover, made no excuses and did not try to cover up. At first he seemed genuinely repentant and willing to submit to the authority of the national ruling elders of his church—the Assemblies of God.

Officials of the Louisiana District Assemblies of God met and determined that Swaggart go through two years of rehabilitation, take three months out of the pulpit in the United States and undergo psychological counseling. More than ten thousand people phoned the Assemblies of God headquarters in Springfield, Missouri, many of them demanding that Swaggart be disciplined according to traditional church regulations. According to the Assemblies of God, any minister guilty of sexual immorality is not to preach for at least one year.

The National Council of the Assemblies of God sent a message to the Louisiana District asking that they reconsider their decision and give Swaggart a stricter sentence. The Louisiana presbyters, however, rejected the National Council's recommendation and sent back their original finding, which called for only a three-month ban on Swaggart's preaching in the United States, with permission to fulfill preaching commitments in foreign countries.

The secular press minced no words in suspecting favoritism and quickly pointed to the $14 million that Swaggart's ministries contributed to the Assemblies of God each year. *Newsweek* reported that the Assemblies of God ". . . can ill afford to lose Swaggart, who supplies a sixth of the denomination's foreign-mission budget and remains the church's most popular evangelist."[9]

But to their credit, national Assemblies of God leaders refused to budge. They held to their decision that Swaggart should undergo two years of rehabilitation and counseling, the first year of which would include staying out of the pulpit and off the air. On March 19, 1988, the National Council overruled the Louisiana District, which then complied "for the sake of unity."[10] Swaggart's church gave him thirty days to agree to the request in writing. If he failed to do so, he could face being defrocked and dismissed from his ministry in the Assemblies of God.

Swaggart's response was immediate. Communicating through his lawyer, he hinted to the Assemblies of God officials that he would reject their discipline and that he still planned to return to the pulpit and his $150 million a year ministry by May 22, 1988—three months after his initial confession of moral wrong-doing.

A few days later, Swaggart sent an official letter to the Assemblies of God declaring he would not submit to their discipline. Left with no other recourse but capitulating to Swaggart's defiance, the Assemblies of God elders held a telephone conference and voted to "dismiss him as an ordained minister of the General Council of the Assemblies of God."[11]

According to statements released by Swaggart, his decision to defy the ruling was deeply influenced by financial concerns. His yearlong absence from public ministry, said Swaggart, would destroy the TV ministry and cause severe problems for the Jimmy Swaggart Bible College.

As he promised, Jimmy Swaggart did return to the pulpit and television on May 22, 1988. He did not confirm or deny the reports of his alleged meetings with prostitutes, but instead referred to his "trying time" and the "leviathan" with which he had struggled in a vivid dream. He said: "Guilt is not of God. When Jesus took the sin away, He took the guilt away as well . . . I lay the guilt at the foot of the Cross. I will never again look at it. I will never again pick it up. I will never again look back."[12]

I'm not sure if Swaggart's defiance of church discipline met with much approval from his sixty-two-year-old Aunt Edna, who lives in Mandeville, Louisiana. *People Weekly* quoted her as saying she was shocked at the news of her nephew's original confession on February 21:

> To tell you the truth, it made me sick. My blood pressure shot way up. But somehow God can take things that are wrong, like this problem, and turn them around to His glory.
>
> If it's true, . . . maybe that's why he preached so hard against it for so long, because he knew what a grip it could get on you. Jimmy's daddy said this might help Jimmy learn not to be so critical of others. I think maybe this will make Jimmy a better man, a more humble minister. Maybe now he won't be so hard on people.
>
> It just goes to show that none of us is so high that we can't fall, and maybe that's what God is trying to show us with this.[13]

William Martin, a Rice University sociologist, who has made a study of TV evangelists, commented in a *People Weekly* interview that in the beginning of Swaggart's public ministry, he thought he was one of the most honest and sincere preachers he had ever met. Over the years, however, Martin believes he saw Swaggart change.

"He really seems to have been seduced by the power and the fame," said Martin. "I think what happens to this kind of person is that he begins to think, 'I couldn't have come this far if not for God.' Then he begins to think, 'Well, if I have this idea to build a Bible college or a mission, it must have come from God.' Next he starts to say, 'God told me this. God told me that.' And the next step from there is that he says, 'I think what God meant to say was. . . .'"[14]

Trust God, Not Your Favorite Celebrity

I tell audiences to enjoy their favorites—in the local pulpit or on TV—and to learn from them, but never worship them as idols. One morning recently, as I read my Bible, 1 Corinthians 2:5 really hit me: In effect Paul says, "Don't let your faith rest on the wisdom of men."

In 1972 I toured the ruins of the early Corinthian church which Paul had founded. It came to me that Christians are always in danger of falling back into idol worship of things we've created instead of worshiping God.

Idol worship happens all around us today. Unfortunately, we even make idols out of some preachers. We really do. And when a preacher falls or something disappointing happens, like a church split, a lot of people crumble. Their faith just falls apart, because it was patterned after the wisdom of men.

God vows, "I will not give my glory to another or my praise to idols" (Isa. 42:8). Movie stars, baseball stars, football stars, stars in ministry—it doesn't matter—any of them can become idols. Respect these people. Enjoy them and benefit from what they do and say, but realize that they still are mere human beings.

Howard Cummings, overseer of missionaries sent out by the Assemblies of God, was recently quoted in *Newsweek*: "There will be a great deal of disillusionment, particularly overseas, where Third World church leaders have looked up to Jimmy Swaggart with almost messianic adoration."[15]

I can only pray that the disillusionment over the failures of Jimmy Swaggart and Jim Bakker will quickly be replaced by remembering and trusting in truth from God's Word. How can we forget that all of us—*including ministers*—are sinners? All of us fall short of God's standards (Rom. 3:23). To admire any person with "messianic adoration" is as sinful as posing as a self-styled messiah. As Donald Miller, a professor of social ethics, recorded in a *Los Angeles Times* editorial, men of God are no more ". . . immune from moral failure than doctors are spared from heart attacks or influenza."[16]

Professor Miller refers to Dostoevsky's insight that we human beings prefer miracle, mystery and authority to God's offer of freedom and faith in the Bible. No wonder, then, that there are overwhelming temptations for people in ministry to start believing their own press clippings and allow adoring audiences to confuse them with the Divine. "The Creator," says Miller, "is not to be mistaken for the creation, and placing ultimate faith in any human form, whether a person or a religious institution, is a form of idolatry."[17]

I did a simple study in the Psalms on the word "trust" and found dozens of verses comparing the folly of trusting in men or what they build and the wisdom in trusting in God. For example:

"Some trust in chariots and some in horses, but we trust in the name of the Lord our God" (ch. 20:7).

"But man, despite his riches, does not endure; he is like the beasts that perish. This is the fate of those that trust in themselves, and of their followers, who approve their sayings" (ch. 49:12–13).

"It is better to take refuge in the Lord than to trust in man. It is better to take refuge in the Lord than to trust in princes" (ch. 118:8–9).

The Bible is full of teachings on trusting God. Proverbs 3:5–6 has reminded millions: "Trust in the Lord with all your heart and lean not on your own understanding; in all your ways acknowledge him, and he will make your paths straight."

Jesus told His followers: "Walk while you have the light, before darkness overtakes you. The man who walks in the dark does not know where he is going. Put your trust in the light while you have it, so that you may become sons of light. . . . Trust in God; trust also in me" (John 12:35b–36; 14:1).

Hollow Answers from a Bruised Reed

Charles Haddon Spurgeon once said there is a vast difference between trusting in broken reeds—weak and sinful human beings—and trusting in the Lord, Who is a "solid pillar sustaining all [our] weight."[18]

As I read different accounts of the falls of Jim Bakker and Jimmy Swaggart, I couldn't help but think of Numbers 32:23: "You may be sure that your sin will find you out." In October 1987, Jimmy Swaggart published a 316-page book he had written entitled *Straight Answers to Tough Questions.* Ironically, many of his "straight" answers dealt with staying sexually and morally pure as he warned against such evils as dancing, movies and television.

In his book, Swaggart wrote that the bottom line for any Christian is that the believer's body is the temple of the Holy Spirit (see 1 Cor. 6:19-20). According to Swaggart: "We are lights in the midst of darkness. We are not our own but are bought with a price—the shed blood of our Lord Jesus Christ at Calvary. We must exemplify righteousness and purity; anything else will lead us or others toward sin."[19]

Swaggart further stated that the Christian life means separation from the world. Christians should stand for something and be sure the world knows ". . . which side we are really on. That is the gospel I preach; that is the way I try to live my life; that is the way I interpret the Bible."[20]

In *Straight Answers*, Swaggart noted that "sex is natural and desirable within the boundaries of marriage. Physical attraction and mating are ordained by God. Men and women are made for marriage. God intended that sex drives be satisfied in the holy communion of wedlock."[21]

The author went on to talk about all the emphasis on sex and pornography in our society today and the perversions Satan has brought into the open. Nonetheless, he challenged, people should never think sexual activity is evil. Sexual needs and desires are perfectly legitimate as long as they are satisfied between husband and wife.[22]

Although Swaggart didn't deal directly with any questions on pornography in *Straight Answers,* he has long been an outspoken foe of pornography in his preaching. Observers of his broadcasts note that as late as December 1987 he was continuing to speak against pornography and the U.S. Supreme Court's lenient rulings on obscenity.[23]

Ironically, the same month Swaggart's book was published, he was confronted by Marvin Gorman, who had received an anonymous telephone tip about Swaggart's contacts with prostitutes. Gorman had Swaggart followed by a private investigator who photographed him leaving a motel with a prostitute. Gorman, who had lost his own pulpit in an Assemblies of God church almost a year before when Swaggart reported Gorman's sexual affairs to church officials, made Swaggart promise to confess to Assemblies of God authorities. And while the minister did confess to his wife and son in October,[24] he delayed talking to church officials until Gorman forced the issue in February 1988. In a ten-hour session with church elders on February 18, Swaggart was confronted by photos of himself in the company of the prostitute. He reportedly admitted to the elders that he had paid her to perform pornographic acts and that pornography had fascinated him ever since he was a young boy.[25]

In sermons preached on television in December 1987, Swaggart described himself as a "poor, pitiful, flawed preacher" and at one point identified himself with Judas. One communications professor who monitors television evangelists has speculated that Swaggart may have been preparing his listeners for the bad news that would inevitably break soon.[26] And break it did—the following February when Marvin Gorman turned him in to church officials.

In *Straight Answers to Tough Questions,* Swaggart defined fornication four different ways: (1) incest or other perversions; (2) repeated adultery; (3) idol worship; and (4) consorting with prostitutes. According to Swaggart, adulterous affairs are not grounds for divorce and every effort should be made to reconcile. If adultery continues, the offended spouse should "forgive again and again."[27]

Human Beings Are So Very Frail

As I read Jimmy Swaggart's book, *Straight Answers to Tough Questions*, I was struck by how right he is about so many things, but how wrong he was living at the time he wrote them. What happened to Jimmy Swaggart is a lesson in human frailty and our susceptibility to sin and hypocrisy. It's a lesson to me about being sure I live the truth that I write about.

When asked about Swaggart's behavior, different psychologists have concurred that he needs long-term therapy, something Swaggart has always disdained, saying that psychology is "of the devil."

How Can Fallen Leaders Be Restored?

Leaders like Jimmy Swaggart and Jim Bakker aren't the only ones who suffer from temptations to stray sexually or start believing their own press kits. There but for trusting and obeying the grace of God go any of us. Other pastors, priests and Christians have fallen into sin of every kind, from having affairs with church secretaries to molesting altar boys.

Should fallen leaders be restored, and if so, how? One of the best discussions of this question I have seen is by Kenneth Kantzer, who wrote in a November 1987 issue of *Christianity Today*: "The church has always dealt more lightly with converted sinners than with backslidden saints."[28] Kantzer lays out several excellent principles for dealing with a fallen leader, including the following:

God may permit a leader to fall into sin in order to help him or her mature or grow in sanctification.
Forgiving a fallen leader doesn't necessarily mean he or she deserves to be restored to leadership—at least right away.

As Kantzer says:

God . . . knows our hearts. Neither at too fast nor too slow a pace will God nudge us back into leadership. In one respect, those who have fallen are like new converts or babes in Christ. They are not to be received immediately into roles of responsible leadership, teaching and governance in the church.[29]

On the part of the fallen leader, there must be remorse, confession, fruits that befit repentance, restitution and retreat from public ministry for a sufficient time. How long is sufficient? That can vary. Kantzer points to the apostle Peter, who waited two months after his fall before he exercised any leadership in the church. On the other hand, Paul spent three years in Arabia after his conversion before he began his missionary journeys.

When a leader does try to return to ministry, he should have, says Kantzer, a genuine call from God. As Kantzer observes:

> God is free to lay his servant "on the shelf" permanently or to call him back. But the call must be accompanied by a clear message to those who are to accept leadership. Neither the repentant sinner nor the church can dictate to God, for he heals in his own time. Just as there is great diversity in the speed with which our physical bodies heal, there is much variation in the time needed for spiritual and emotional healing. We must wait patiently on God for his guidance.[30]

Weariness Can Distort Judgment

Patience has marked the restoration of Gordon MacDonald, another Christian leader who fell in 1987. In June of that year, MacDonald resigned his presidency of InterVarsity Christian Fellowship, "for personal reasons, having been involved in an adulterous relationship in late 1984 and 1985." Long before his resignation, he had broken off the relationship, confessed to his wife and received her forgiveness. He had also submitted himself to the discipline of three trusted Christian leaders. MacDonald hoped that his tragedy was over, but news of his affair was spread through anonymous letters sent to several Christian publishers accusing him of adultery. Once the story became public, MacDonald felt it best that he resign.

In an interview with *Christianity Today*, Gordon MacDonald shared that since 1982 he had become "desperately weary," spiritually as well as physically. He realized that "satan's ability to distort the heart and mind is beyond belief." MacDonald assumes full responsibility for what he did but knows he entered an illicit affair with a friend in 1984 by making decisions out of a distorted heart.[31]

After his resignation from InterVarsity, MacDonald and his wife, Gail, renewed membership at Grace Chapel, Lexington, Mass., where he had been senior pastor until 1984. For the next ten months, he submitted to additional discipline and counsel from the Grace Chapel board of elders. Except for a few speaking engagements to small groups, mostly pastors, MacDonald was not allowed to do any public ministry during his time of discipline. According to the chairman of the elders sub-committee which counseled MacDonald, he battled through overwhelming guilt to a true sense of forgiveness.

On May 1, 1988, MacDonald was recommissioned to public ministry in a special service before 1200 church members and friends. During a thirty-minute address to the congregation, he said, ". . . I'm very sorry I let you down. Perhaps the worst kind of brokenness is the brokenness of being an utter failure because of some bad choices you have made in your life."[32]

During the months of seclusion and quiet, MacDonald and his wife developed a ministry of intercession, praying daily for a long list of people broken by sin and pain. Following the recommissioning service, MacDonald said he might take an official position some day if God seemed to lead, but leadership was not his chief goal. He said, ". . . The only thing I want to do is be a servant."

The Need for Accountability

One other important principle in restoring any fallen leader is accountability. Pastors, evangelists, missionaries—leaders of any kind—must be accountable to responsible Christian peers, not only in spiritual matters but in financial arenas as well. Gordon MacDonald admitted that he lacked mutual accountability through personal friendships. He told *Christianity Today*, "We need friendships where one man regularly looks another man in the eye and asks hard questions about our moral life, our lust, our ambitions, our ego."[33]

MacDonald's words apply to all fallen leaders. As Kenneth Kantzer has pointed out, there have been too many cases where leaders of parachurch organizations will choose board members who are personal friends or relatives. "These hand-picked boards," insisted Kantzer, "do not effectively guard the resources of the kingdom."[34]

Terry Muck believes television evangelists should submit to the kind of checks and balances system commonly found in secular TV:

> With rare exceptions, secular television personalities have little to say about programming. Producers do that. And producers are accountable to programmers and boards of directors. This natural system of checks and balances prevents one man or woman from inappropriately dominating the content of secular programs. Similar checks in religious television will help prevent ministers from becoming more important than ministry.[35]

One More Important Principle

Beyond the principles listed above is one more that I believe is the most important of all. *Sin is a disease more deadly than any virus.* It is easy to shake our heads over the failures and hypocrisy of fallen leaders and then go right on avoiding facing our own shortcomings. If we are to deal with and prevent celebrityism from destroying our leaders and their ministries, we must first look within our own hearts. Shakespeare was no writer of Scripture, but these words from "Julius Caesar" have a prophetic ring for evangelicals today: "The fault, dear Brutus, is not in our stars, but in ourselves . . . ."[36]

No one mounts the pedestal of celebrityism without a big boost from star gazers who raise him or her too high for everyone's own good. There has been much talk of a "house cleaning" that needs to be done among televangelists and other ministries. But by far the most important house cleaning is to be done in my heart and in yours.

In an editorial in *University Magazine* (formerly *His*), Editor Verne Becker points out that we can contribute to the downfall of our leaders by idealizing them too much. The higher we raise them on the pedestal, the easier it is not to bother to pray for them. After all, why would such strong and powerful leaders need our prayers? Becker believes that when leaders fall we must pray for them, love them, forgive them and try to restore them. Above all, we must avoid condemnation, because the next person to fall could easily be one of us.

A third point Becker makes is that we must be careful not to become cynical when leaders do fail. God and His grace are much greater than any individual, and He continues to love and work through all Christians despite their failures.

Becker sums up his editorial by saying we all can have role models or heroes who can be positive influences in our lives, but ". . . we cannot forget that all such people who have ever lived, except one, have been flawed. Jesus is and must always be our only perfect role model; let's look to him first, rather than to models of clay."[37]

The Undertow of Narcissism

Dr. Jon Johnston believes that "evangelicals are being swept away by our society's undertow of narcissism."[38] The apostle Paul warned Timothy that "in the last days, people will be lovers of themselves . . . boastful, proud . . . having a form of godliness but denying its power" (2 Tim. 3:2–5).

Johnston also quotes Joseph Newton, a little-known preacher of the past, whose words fit us perfectly today: "There is a tedious egotism in our day . . . men are self-centered, . . . self-obsessed, and unable to *get themselves off their hands.*"[39]

Sin—the lust of the flesh, the lust of the eye and the pride of life—is an overwhelming force. The only power that can conquer it is God's redemptive love and forgiveness. I thank God for the day He got Dale Evans off her own hands and into His.

For years I struggled with my ego, trying my best to be a star. Oh, in public life I put on what I thought was a "happy face," but inside I was miserable. Nothing of the world was ever enough to satisfy my deepest longing. My steps were uncertain because I was unsure of the right path for my life. I was desperate in my spirit. And then came that wonderful day when I asked God to fill my life.

As the years have rolled on, the star of Jesus grows ever brighter to me. To follow His star is exciting, meaningful and joyous, in spite of difficulties and seeming setbacks.

Backstage in auditoriums, concert halls, TV and motion picture studios, the largest and best-appointed dressing room usually has a big star on the door. This room is reserved for the performer who is "top banana" in the program. Today my preference is the Star of Hope imprinted on my heart, for it is the glory of Christ that gives the greatest fulfillment for my soul.

There are those in show business who call me a "religionist" because of my outspoken witness to the power of Christ in my life. If there is any "star quality" in me at all, it is because the Star of stars has shone in my heart. You see the Bible says, "God is no respecter of persons" (Acts 10:34, KJV). God looks upon the heart for star quality—and only He can put it there. In the next several chapters, we will look at ways we can cooperate with God and make Jesus the only Star in our lives.

Part II

How Can We
Change?

Following Christ—
the only Star

6

Everybody's Somebody
in God's Sight

Years ago when I came to Hollywood, I got to know a supporting actor named Chick Chandler because he and I had the same agent. Chick's wife, Jean, told me what happened at a premiere showing of one of his films.

It seems that Jean dressed in her finest gown and Chick was in his standard tux for a special occasion in Hollywood. But somehow in the crush of the crowd and the blinding spotlights, they got separated, and as Jean frantically looked for her husband in the wild melee, a woman rushed up to her and said, "Are you anybody?"

Jean looked at her and said, "No, are you?"

This story is good for a chuckle, but it also points to why celebrityism grips so many lives. There is an astounding lack of self-esteem in many people who try to fill the void in their lives by worshiping their favorite star or celebrity. Somehow if they can say they met someone who is "somebody," that will make them "somebody," too. And if they can't meet them or get their autograph, they can at least vicariously share in the spotlight by idolizing a favorite star's achievements.

81

Either a Star or a Nobody?

In his excellent book, *Will Evangelicalism Survive Its Own Popularity?* Dr. Jon Johnston, Sociology Professor at Pepperdine University, devotes an entire chapter to "celebrityism." He observes that ". . . many people value an attitude, idea or opinion just because a celebrity expressed it."[1]

Johnston goes on to discuss our American mania for enshrining our national celebrities in Halls of Fame. In fact, we have a Hall of Fame for just about everyone—even animal stars. According to Johnston, there are 750 Halls of Fame in America, while the rest of the world boasts only three.[2]

Johnston wonders what all the fanfare over stars and celebrities is actually saying about the 99.9 percent of the people who never reach stardom. He quotes Mark Bennett, director of "A Chorus Line," who said, "Either you're a star or you're nobody."[3]

Bennett is wrong, of course, and so is all this hoopla over stars and so-called celebrities. Society has gotten completely away from healthy respect for actors, athletes, leaders and achievers of all kinds. It has all turned into a sideshow. Today we make celebrities out of terrorists, assassins, Wall Street inside traders, mass murderer/rapists and vigilantes who take the law into their own hands.

The worship of the famous is what one thinker called ". . . the perversion of the natural human instinct for validation and attention."[4] True, we all need to feel significant and to know our life has meaning. In our high tech culture with TV commercials blasting twenty-four hours a day, computers calling us up with fabulous offers, and junk mail arriving by the ton, it is easy to feel as if you are being folded, stapled and mutilated. As Jon Johnston says, "It's no wonder a lot of people feel processed and 'thing-afied' in our impersonal society."[5]

The caseload of many psychologists or counselors includes patients with some kind of "identity crisis"—people who say, "I have no significance . . . . what can I do? . . . I'm nobody."

Perhaps a lack of identity is one reason why so many people pursue success so fervently. There is no question that success is one of the primary goals of most Americans. Certain surveys and polls may have people saying they value family and friendships more than money, but money is still very, very popular. Money means power, prestige, comfort, pleasure and above all, security.

My Self-Image Plummeted below Zero

I understand the need for security because I sought it and fought for it for many years. When Tom's father deserted us, I was devastated. A fifteen-year-old child myself, I saw my self-image plunge out of sight and my self-esteem drop way below zero. I refused to give Tom up and swore I would make a comfortable and secure life for both of us without help from any man.

In those early years in Hollywood, when I was trying to "make it big" in pictures, Tom and I went to church and I became quite convicted of my grasping way. But then I was grasping for more than fame. I also wanted security for Tom and me because of the way his father had abandoned us.

For the next twenty years I had a real chip on my shoulder. When I began working in Hollywood film studios, my schedules were incredibly long and hard. Tom watched me take pills to go to sleep, pills to wake up—push, push, push, push. He knew what a trap I was in.

Before Christ took over my life, I was like a lot of women I see today who want to "have it all." They try to find themselves by going in all directions. Preoccupation with self turns into narcissism—self-love. You can get so wrapped up in "finding yourself" that you become just like Narcissus—the character in Greek mythology who starved to death gazing at his own reflection in a pool of water. We can become spiritually starved and confused by all the talk of "I'm okay, you're okay," and of being your own "best friend." The truth is, we know we're *not* okay. And we don't feel loved or lovable in a world that is always competitive and often a jungle.

In his excellent book on self-esteem, *Hide or Seek*, Dr. James Dobson says the "gold coin of human worth" is beauty. We all learn this as young as preschool years when adults unconsciously treat the cute, pretty children more nicely than those who are not so noticeable. Dobson says, "The pretty child is much more likely to see the world as warm and accepting; the ugly child is far better acquainted with the cold, steel eyes of rejection."[6]

I was glad to see an interview with Kellye Cash, Miss America 1987, that revealed she was a committed, evangelical Christian. In that interview, Kellye stressed values like refusing to engage in premarital sex, not using abortion to bail yourself out of an unwanted pregnancy, refusing to use drugs and wanting someday to marry a Christian man.

In a sidebar article appearing with Kellye's interview, Don McCrory observed that the nation, young and old alike, pursues the god of beauty with incredible devotion. We even call persons like Kellye "beautiful people." But while the "beautiful people" are admired and some even go on to celebrity status, McCrory reminds his readers that beauty is only skin deep. Real beauty is different and lies deep beneath the skin, unaffected by wrinkles and other imperfections.

McCrory writes, "Of course, beauty which is real and lasting has much more to do with what the eye cannot see than with what it can . . . . lasting beauty even today is that which is cultivated by a right relationship with God. It carries distinct spiritual dimensions. While we cannot, and assuredly should not, dismiss the value of physical beauty, it surely must be kept in proper perspective . . . ."

McCrory concluded his article by quoting Proverbs: "Charm is deceptive and beauty is fleeting; but a woman who fears the Lord is to be praised" (ch. 31:30). He noted that the world would praise Miss America for her beauty, but he wondered if a more enduring characteristic shouldn't be our guide.[7]

Besides being attractive enough to become Miss America, Kellye Cash has some of those "more enduring characteristics" that come from within. During the interview she talked freely about the importance of her personal Christian faith. She related that her family, as beautiful and loving as they are, fail her at times, and friends fail also; but Christ is the One who always pulls her through the hardest places. When asked by the Miss America judges to list her best qualities, she named her ability to forgive:

"And that is because of the love I have for God, and the love that he has for me helps me to have love for others."[8]

Until I allowed Christ to take over my life and become my Lord, I operated on the world's perspective of worth. I worried constantly about how pretty I was, how well I could sing, how I was coming across, what kind of an impression I was making. But as soon as Christ came in, I got a very different perspective. My self-esteem didn't depend on how the world treated me; it depended on God, Who had made me in the first place and loved me enough to die for me. For the first time I could love myself in the right way and feel real love, not merely a hunger for something that always seemed just out of reach.

Is It Okay to "Love Yourself"?

There is a lot of misunderstanding about loving yourself. Some Christians believe even thinking the thought is sinful, but I don't agree. One reason we find it hard to love ourselves is that we grow up getting the opposite idea. We are often harder on ourselves than anyone else.

As Lloyd Ogilvie writes, "If we treated our friends the way we treat ourselves, putting down strengths and touting mistakes, we wouldn't have any friends left." Lloyd shares an experience he had while alone in his study that taught him a new level of the power of self-acceptance. He was trying to write a chapter on the problem of self-estrangement and how it can fill one's life with fear. While he assumed he had healthy self-esteem, he could not get the chapter going.

Finally he heard the Lord in his thoughts, telling him to close his eyes and form an image of himself. But somehow he just couldn't form that image. He realized he had been so busy he had been out of touch with himself and despite all his ministry and work for others, out of touch with God. He realized he needed a fresh experience of what he advised on his own television program —"Let God Love You!"

As he enjoyed a fresh touch of God's unqualified love, he started to get an image of himself as a loved and joyous person.

And then the Lord put another thought into his mind: "Lloyd, go put your arms around yourself. Actually, picture your punitive self embracing your struggling self."

Lloyd objected and told God that wouldn't be easy. What about all of his faults and insufficiencies?

But when the Lord commanded, "Do it!" Lloyd obeyed. He writes: "As I dared to embrace myself in an extension of the Lord's gracious embrace, I felt a deeper self-acceptance than ever before. A profound inner peace flooded me, followed by a new resiliency and freedom. With tears streaming down my face, I sat there praising the Lord that in spite of everything, I could be a priest to myself. I could offer Christ's love, forgiveness and acceptance to the needy person inside."[9]

Lloyd cautions his readers that he isn't advocating some kind of narcissistic form of self-centeredness. He believes that "the final link in experiencing Christ-centered, Cross-oriented healing grace is to fully embrace ourselves."[10] He quotes Paul, who said he was one of the least of the apostles and not worthy to be called an apostle because he persecuted the church of God. Paul went on to affirm, however: "But by the grace of God I am what I am: and his grace which was bestowed upon me was not in vain; but I labored more abundantly than they all: yet not I, but the grace of God which was with me" (1 Cor. 15:10, KJV).

As a Christian, I can love and embrace myself because of God's grace and for no other reason. I can accept and take care of myself for Him and through Him. I don't love myself because I am a self-made person; I can love myself because God made me and redeemed me. I *know* I am significant and that my life has meaning. And I want the praise to go to Him, and to *no one else.*

A "Put Down" from Dick Halverson

When I became a Christian, I became involved with the Hollywood Christian group formed by Dr. Henrietta Mears. Many musical people, including opera singer Jerome Hines, met in her home on Stone Canyon Drive in Bel Air. Connie Haines was a member, and so was Tim Spencer, one of The Sons of the Pioneers, who wrote "Room Full of Roses." Tim was our first executive director.

Later Dick Halverson became executive director and our "chaplain" of sorts. Before Dick became a Christian, he used to sing with dance bands. One night he sang for the Hollywood Christian group and his song—actually it was a hymn—was so lovely, it just knocked me out.

I had no idea Dick could sing so beautifully. Afterward I went up to him and wanted to tell him how much I appreciated his song because I had been a band singer for so many years myself. I said, "Dick, that was simply great. I didn't know you could sing like that."

Halverson, who today is Chaplain of the United States Senate, looked me right in the eye, never cracked a smile and said, "Praise *the Lord.*"

Because I was a new Christian and didn't really understand, I thought, "What's the matter with this guy? Can't he take a compliment? What is he, some kind of nut?" I really felt put down at the time, but later I understood exactly what Dick was saying. You don't take compliments for yourself, because anything you do is for God's glory, not yours.

Rhonda Fleming Put God in Charge

In recent months I have been doing an interview show called "A Date with Dale" on the TBN television network, which originates out of Tustin, California, just south of Los Angeles. My guests, often from the entertainment field, share how Christ has made the difference in their lives. Among the many actors, actresses, singers, composers and other highly visible personalities who have appeared is Rhonda Fleming.

An accomplished singer who has made numerous appearances in stage musicals and concerts, Rhonda is probably best remembered as an actress who did forty motion pictures, including "Spellbound," "A Connecticut Yankee in King Arthur's Court," "Gunfight at the OK Corral" and "Pony Express." Among her co-stars have been Gregory Peck, Robert Mitchum, Kirk Douglas,

Charlton Heston, Glenn Ford, Burt Lancaster, Bob Hope, Bing Crosby and Ronald Reagan, with whom she made four films.

While discussing the inherent tensions of her profession, Rhonda told me: "An actress is a commodity and must sell that commodity to the industry and the public. You can become so obsessed with yourself, so involved with yourself, that it can easily become a 'me first' situation. Somewhere along the line you have to be shaken up and brought to your knees and realize that you must put God first. Depending upon God instead of our own resources brings a healthy self-confidence as we release God-given talents to Him for His purpose and for our highest fulfillment."

While still a teenager, Rhonda accepted Christ at the Forest Home (California) Christian Conference Center, which was founded by Dr. Henrietta Mears. Whenever she started floundering spiritually, she went back to Forest Home for refreshment, and also spent time in Dr. Mears' home as part of the Hollywood Christian group. She is thankful that "Christ always kept His arms around me. Somehow I didn't get too far astray."

Rhonda recalls being approached by a Hollywood agent while dashing to one of her high school classes. She referred him to her mother and the end result was that she was placed under a seven-year contract to David O. Selznick's studio and thrust into acting right out of high school, with no background or experience whatsoever.

"I remember those early days," she says. "There were a lot of opportunities offered that might have been steppingstones to incredible films, but I didn't take them because I just wasn't to do it. I was protected in many ways."

Rhonda recalls not associating a great deal with stars, producers or directors. She preferred the "little people" whom she discovered were Christians—grips, cameramen, makeup persons and hairdressers. She loved to talk with them because she always had that hunger to share.

Rhonda is now a member of a prayer group that meets each Thursday in the home of John and Bonnie Green in Beverly Hills. Throughout her career she has depended heavily on Christian fellowship and teaching to counteract the pull of celebrityism. "At the time you don't realize it's happening," she explains. "It's very subtle. You walk into the room and it's like the light is on you. But the constant attention and high profile publicity make it difficult to keep the correct balance.

"Obviously, to be an actor or actress you need a certain amount of healthy ego and a certain amount of self-involvement so you can make the most of putting yourself into your roles. But it must all be for His glory. When we allow God to fully take charge of our lives and let Him lead and direct us—we keep our eyes on the real Star, not ourselves!"[11]

God's Love Produces Change

I identify very well with Rhonda's insights. For years I was a willing participant in a celebrity system totally predicated on feeding the human ego. But after I gave my life to Christ, I realized I wasn't anything except what He was in me. He was there to use me and develop me. That's what helped cure my stagefright, insecurity and fear of how I was coming across.

I like what Pete Gillquist wrote in his book, *Fresh Insight Into Love Is Now*: "The end result of God's love flowing unconditionally from Him to us is that a love response is activated within our lives. His love becomes creative; it molds us into new persons. God's love does not *demand* a change; it *produces* one."[12]

I think many Christians, in particular, are confused by what it means to "love your neighbor as you love yourself" and what it means to have an ego. There is nothing wrong with loving yourself in the right way. As Tom Skinner once said, "If you can't love yourself, your neighbor is in big trouble!"

Whenever we talk about the ego, it is usually in a negative way. We say someone is egotistical, or has a big ego, or is taking an ego trip. What we mean is, someone is putting too much importance on himself, becoming conceited, overbearing, greedy, selfish, and so on.

Actually, the ego is a psychological term for the center of the personality. There is nothing wrong with having a healthy ego, because a healthy ego doesn't make you conceited or overbearing at all; in fact, it makes you modest, kind and accepting of others because you aren't running scared out of insecurity or an inferiority complex.

I like what Billy Graham says about God not asking us to get rid of our ego. "In fact," says Billy, "it is important for us to have a right understanding of our value and importance—what the psychologists call a healthy self-image. But we develop that best when we begin to see ourselves as God sees us—as persons who are so valuable to Him that He wants us to be forgiven and cleansed of sin so we can be His children."[13]

Or as Pete Gillquist puts it: ". . . in conversion, my ego acquires a forwarding address. I am no longer under the domain of the flesh; I am now controlled by the Holy Spirit. The real me is a new person; I have been reborn."[14]

No one has improved on how the apostle Paul said it: "Therefore, if anyone is in Christ, he is a new creation; the old is gone, the new has come!" (2 Cor. 5:17).

When we see ourselves as God sees us—as new creations reconciled to Him, with our sins no longer counted against us, we can love and accept ourselves for who we really are.

Where the Cure Has to Begin

In 1980 Jon Johnston wrote: "To shatter the chains of celebrityism, evangelicals must begin practicing a radically new approach to judging human worth. Ironically, this radical new approach is as old as the teachings of Scripture."[15]

In other words, every person needs to realize his or her worth in God's sight. If we want to cure celebrityism, that's where it has to begin.

According to Dr. Maurice Wagner, the Christian with healthy self-esteem and a sound self-image enjoys three basic feelings or emotions: belongingness, worthiness and competence. Wagner says these feelings are like three tones of a musical chord, and the first note—*belongingness*—is vital to the other two.[16]

All of us want to belong—somewhere and to someone. To

belong is to be aware of being wanted and accepted, cared for and enjoyed. In today's parlance, we call it "being in."

There is no more important task for parents than to make their children feel accepted, to make them know that they belong and are loved. My parents did their best to give me that feeling, and they were always there to pick me up, take me back and get me on my feet again. But I was so full of rebellion that they couldn't protect me from myself. Marrying at age fourteen and having a child at age fifteen and then being deserted were experiences which left me feeling that I didn't belong anywhere. For many years I struggled with feelings of not being accepted, of having to earn my way, of being on the outside always looking in. But when I gave my life entirely to Christ, I knew I *belonged*. I was finally home. I was loved and accepted.

When we build on feelings of belongingness and acceptance, we develop *worthiness*, which has to do with feelings of being "right and good," feelings that "I count." When we lack the vital emotion of worthiness, we become defensive, angry, hostile. We try to rationalize and justify our actions by countering, "You don't understand. . . ."

For years, "You don't understand" was one of my favorite phrases. I lacked feelings of worthiness, and guilt ate at me constantly. I didn't feel I was right, because I knew I hadn't done what was right. When my first husband, also a teenager, deserted me and my son, I felt I had goofed. I had disobeyed my parents and greatly disappointed them. Instead of turning to Christ, I turned inward. I was determined to prove I was desirable, attractive, capable and talented. I would show the world my first husband had been wrong to leave me. I wanted to make something of myself, as well as to give Tom an opportunity to be somebody.

But my efforts netted only more and more struggle, more doubts about my worth. Only when I turned to the Lord and admitted my brokenness and asked Him to take the broken pieces, glue me back together and use me as He saw fit, did I find peace. I can say from personal experience that the only way to have true feelings of worthiness is to give your life completely to Christ. He is the One Who makes us righteous. And only because of His righteousness can we feel right or good about ourselves.

The third basic feeling of good self-esteem is *competence* — "I can do it!" Competence makes us feel adequate, courageous, hopeful and strong enough to face whatever life brings our way. Obviously, success builds our feelings of competence, and failure tears them down.

Again, I see so clearly how my struggles before Christ came into my life reflected my lack of feeling real confidence. My stagefright on the Chase and Sanborn Hour, never feeling secure or good enough, were indications of low self-esteem. I always felt threatened because I didn't think I performed well enough to gain approval. I had no inner resources to handle my failures, which always seemed much greater than any of my successes.

But Christ changed all that. I finally realized I belonged to Him and that He made me worthy and "good enough." I didn't have to depend on what "they" thought. After I knew what Christ thought, I relaxed and felt competent and capable to do my best.

God Meets Our Basic Needs

Psychologists have different lists of "basic human needs." Larry Crabb, a Christian counselor, says two of our most basic ones are security and significance. In other words, we need to feel safe and know that our lives do matter. Unfortunately, we can search for significance and security in all the wrong places, forgetting that God meets both these needs more than adequately.

As I have searched the Scriptures for the best description of how God meets our need for significance, I find one passage that says it especially well.[17] First Corinthians 3:16–23 gives me three wonderful reasons for feeling significant in God's sight:

God's Spirit lives in me.

I am God's special possession and live under His protection.

God has given me all I need.

I don't think it is a coincidence that Paul shares these concepts with the church at Corinth, which was torn apart by its own celebrity system. Part of the church made Peter the star, while others lifted Apollos high on the celebrity pedestal. And of course, some worshiped Paul, who let them know that no one deserved worship but Christ. Paul asked the erring Corinthian Christians, "Is Christ divided? Was Paul crucified for you? Were you baptized into the name of Paul?" (1 Cor. 1:13).

Later in this letter, Paul tells the Corinthians that their celebrityism has forced him to say he can't address them as spiritual, ". . . but as worldly—mere infants in Christ . . . . For when one says, 'I follow Paul,' and another, 'I follow Apollos,' are you not mere men? What, after all, is Apollos? And what is Paul? Only servants, through whom you came to believe—as the Lord has assigned to each his task. I planted the seed, Apollos watered it, but God made it grow" (1 Cor. 3:1, 4–6).

A few verses later, Paul gives reasons that Christians should not play earthly favorites but should have a healthy self-concept built on finding significance in Christ alone. *The Living Bible* puts it clearly: "Don't you realize that all of you together are the house of God, and that the Spirit of God lives among you in his house? If anyone defiles and spoils God's home, God will destroy him. For God's home is holy and clean, and you are that home" (1 Cor. 3:16–17, TLB).

Two powerful self-image builders are in these verses:

1. God's Spirit lives in the Christian.

2. The Christian is God's special possession and lives under His protection.

God actually lives inside you and me! That's a mind-boggling thought I can't forget. Next time you feel unimportant and insignificant, remember where God lives. Nothing Christians do is insignificant. God lives in us and He works through us. When we pray, He acts. God could have chosen to live anywhere, yet He chose to live within the people He redeemed at such terrible cost.

Paul goes on to tell us we're God's special possession, living under His protection. If Christians are harmed, God takes it personally! Remember when Paul (then he was Saul the Pharisee) headed for Damascus to persecute more Christians? When Christ appeared to him in a blinding flash on the road, He didn't ask, "Why are you persecuting My people?" Instead, He said, "Saul,

Saul, why do you persecute *Me?*" Saul's immediate reply was, "Who are you, *Lord?*" Paul's life was changed in a moment when he heard the answer: "I am Jesus, whom you are persecuting" (see Acts 9:4–5).

Paul got the message. By persecuting Christians, he was persecuting Jesus Himself. I don't have any way of proving it, but I wouldn't be surprised if Paul wasn't thinking about that Damascus Road conversation with Jesus when he wrote to the Corinthians and told them the Spirit of God lived within their very bodies.

A few years ago, a film came out called "My Bodyguard." The plot revolved around a high school student who, because of his small size, was being terrorized and blackmailed by a class bully. The smaller fellow decided to hire a huge student to be his personal bodyguard. In one sense, verse seventeen sounds as if we can call God our Bodyguard. If anyone destroys God's temple (us), God will destroy him!

I believe, however, that the real emphasis in this verse is upon God's personal interest in every Christian. The One who spoke and created the universe also sent His Son to die for us. How can we possibly be insignificant? Christians cost God far too much to ever be insignificant!

God Makes Us Capable

The third great truth in Paul's letter to the Corinthians is that God not only lives in us, and takes special interest in us, but He also gives us all we need to live competently and confidently in this world. Paul told the Corinthians they shouldn't be proud of following the "wise men of this world" (celebrityism again!). The wisdom of the world is just so much foolishness to God. Men have always stumbled over their own "wise schemes" and fallen flat on their faces (see 1 Cor. 3:18–20). We shouldn't ever glory in men—that is, look to them as stars, celebrities or miracle workers who have given us significance and security because they're charming or talented.

Paul told the Corinthians:

> For God has already given you everything you need. He has given
> you Paul and Apollos and Peter as your helpers. He has given you
> the whole world to use, and life and even death are your servants.
> He has given you all of the present and all of the future. All are
> yours, and you belong to Christ, and Christ is God's (1 Cor.
> 3:21–23, TLB).

We don't have Paul, Apollos or Peter around to help us
today in person, but we do have their writings to guide and teach
us. As William Barclay observes, Paul tells the Corinthians that by
having all these factions and this party spirit based on loyalty to
certain stars and celebrities in their midst, they are making a
horrendous mistake. Instead of being content with being held in
God's hands and kept under His protection, they are seeking to
"give themselves over into the hands of some man." He continues, "This identification with some party is the acceptance of
slavery by those who should be kings. In point of fact, they are
masters of all things, because they belong to Christ and Christ
belongs to God."[18]

In summary, Christians don't need to be star gazers or star
worshipers. I like the way Lloyd Ogilvie put it on one of his
telecasts. I recall he emphasized that everybody is a celebrity—
everybody. You celebrate a person's birthday, homecomings. You
celebrate together Thanksgiving and Christmas. You celebrate
high school graduation. Everybody is a celebrity and everybody is
a V.I.P. to God!

It's just like what Jesus said about going after one sheep even
though ninety-nine others were safe.

It's doubtful that anyone will ever rush up to you and say,
"Quick, tell me, are you anybody?" but if that ever happens, you
can declare, "Absolutely! I belong to God. He dwells in me and is
interested in my every move. Every Christian is somebody in
God's eyes because every Christian belongs to Christ, and Christ
is God's!"

7

Live—Don't Just Talk—Humility

As we seek positive ways to deal with celebrityism, we must not overlook that elusive quality called humility. Even more important, we need to recognize the flip side of humility—pride—which is such a pervasive part of the celebrity syndrome.

When I think of humility I'm always reminded of experiences wherein God took my pride down a peg or two by reminding me of how weak and human I really am. Paul said, "Do not think of yourself more highly than you ought, but rather think of yourself with sober judgment . . . ." (Rom. 12:3). I'm not sure exactly what Paul meant by "sober judgment," but I do know he meant I shouldn't take myself too seriously.

One Sunday I decided to wear a new dress and, because we were running late, I took it out of the box, hurriedly put it on and rushed off to church.

As I was hurrying down the aisle to my seat, I suddenly felt a tapping on my shoulder. It was an usher, a man who is a good friend of ours. I started to wonder, "What is the matter anyway? What are you doing?" Just as I was getting ready to sit down, he did something with the back of my dress. Quickly he leaned over and said, "Your price tag was hanging out." Everybody nearby chuckled with laughter, and a lady sitting behind me whispered in my ear, "Dale, you can call this your Minnie Pearl dress. You know—Minnie Pearl with the price tag on her hat?"

It seemed as if people were giggling all over the church. It was a light colored dress, pastel, but the price tag was bright orange, so it really stood out. Years ago, before I gave my life to the Lord, if someone had discovered a price tag hanging out of my dress I would have been so mortified I would have just gone into hiding for two or three days. But I can laugh about that story and tell it on myself when I speak, because Christ has taught me not to take myself too seriously. Once He came in, I learned what Paul knew so well, "By the grace of God I am what I am, and He will use whatever is there."

How Not to Define Humility

There are many good definitions of humility, but one of my favorites is "getting your eyes off yourself and putting them on Christ." A lot of Christians mistakenly think "being humble" means groveling around, toe in the sand, apologizing for being alive. Self-deprecation isn't humility; it's poor self-esteem all dressed up and looking for someone who will notice.

It's likely you have complimented another Christian for giving a devotional or singing a solo and then heard the person say, "It wasn't me; it was the Lord," or "I didn't do it; the Holy Spirit did." Sometimes people say things like that because they are honestly thanking God for working through what talent or energy they have dedicated to Him. But when words like "It wasn't me; it was the Holy Spirit" are said self-effacingly to make sure others know we are humble, we aren't humble at all. The truth is, it's possible to take great pride in being humble!

In his letter to the church at Colossae, Paul spoke of proud men who claimed to be humble. They kept all kinds of rules that required strong devotion and regulations which were even humiliating and hard on the body, but their discipline didn't help them conquer evil thoughts and desires. All this "humility" only made them proud (see Col. 2:16-23).

Paul's words remind me of Golda Meir, former Prime

Minister of Israel, who was talking to someone who was groveling in false humility. Tersely she put the man in his place by saying, "Quit trying to be so humble. You're not that great."

The point is, humility demands honesty. J. B. Phillips translates Romans 12:3 like this: "Don't cherish exaggerated ideas of yourself or your importance, but try to have a sane estimate of your capabilities by the light of the faith that God has given to you all."

Some people are constantly putting themselves down, talking about how they could have done something better, how they're really not fit for this or that. This isn't humility—in many cases it's a low self-image or a form of concealed pride.

Celebrityism Feeds on Pride

Any system of star worshiping is built on a foundation of pride, and not just on the part of the stars who get all puffed up with big doses of attention. Adoring fans who worship them are not admiring out of humble devotion; they are looking for a vicarious way to experience power and success.

Pride is closely related to power, as we can see in a character called Lucifer. While Isaiah (see ch. 14) is referring to the earthly ruler of Babylon and predicting his downfall, many of the verses in this passage contain such imagery and symbolism that conservative Bible scholars believe they suggest a sinister figure lurking in the background who is the power and motivation behind the godless defiance and rebellion of Babylon. In other words, Satan himself.

Ironically, the Hebrew word translated Lucifer means "shining one." The New King James Bible translates verse 12 this way: "How you are fallen from heaven, O Lucifer, son of the morning!" The New American Standard Bible says: "How you have fallen from heaven, O star of the morning, son of the dawn!"

The term "shining one" refers to Satan's origin, when he was the brightest and first among God's angels, so bright that Isaiah refers to him as a morning star. One commentator says this "speaks of the light that was his character and his abode before the blackness of sin invaded and surrounded him."[1]

We learn more about Lucifer from another prophet, Ezekiel,

who prophesied against the godless city of Tyre and its ruler. In chapter 28, Ezekiel refers to a "guardian cherub" who is "the model of perfection, full of wisdom and perfect in beauty" (see v. 12). Some scholars feel that, while Ezekiel is talking primarily about the king of Tyre, he is also making references to a being who is far more powerful than any human—Satan.

Cherubim were the highest classification of angelic beings, created specifically to represent God's presence, glory, holiness and sovereignty. Not only that, but Satan appears to have had first rank among all other created creatures. Terms like "anointed cherub," and "covering cherub" point to his high position as literally a guardian for God.[2]

But the guardian cherub Lucifer fell. More precisely, he was kicked out of heaven. His crime? He wasn't satisfied with being called a morning star and a model of perfection, full of wisdom and perfect in beauty. He wasn't satisfied with being God's anointed guardian. He wanted it all. He wanted to be the *only* star. He was cast down to the earth because he said in his heart, "I will ascend to heaven; I will raise my throne above the stars of God; I will sit enthroned on the mount of assembly, on the utmost heights of the sacred mountain. I will ascend above the tops of the clouds; I will make myself like the Most High" (Isa. 14:13–14).

That final phrase, "like the Most High," is the clincher. Instead of submitting to God's will, he wanted to usurp God's authority. But that is impossible. You can't be like God and still let God be God because there is none like Him. God will not share His glory with anyone (see Isa. 42:8; 43:10; 44:6).

Lucifer's pride made him thirst for power. Pride and power always go together. Richard Foster writes:

> Power can destroy or create. The power that destroys demands ascendancy; it demands total control. It destroys relationship; it destroys trust; it destroys dialogue; it destroys integrity. And this is true whether we look through the macrocosm of human history or the microcosm of our own personal history.[3]

Foster believes the sin of Adam and Eve in the Garden was their lust for power. Satan had let the serpent talk them into wanting all knowledge and to be like God. It makes sense that he would tempt Adam and Eve with the very same sin that got him thrown out of heaven, doesn't it? At the bottom line, pride is wanting to be God and have His power.

A thirst for power is what caused the disciples to argue bitterly over who would be greatest in God's kingdom. And they argued more than once, because this same argument comes up in all four gospels. Richard Foster observes that whenever we argue over who will be greatest, we are also deciding who will be least. Nobody wants to be least. We all want to be at the top of the heap, on the highest rung of the ladder.

Jesus Turned "Greatness" Upside Down

Jesus must have grown weary of the disciples' arguments over who was greatest. On two different occasions James and John approached Him specifically and wanted Him to grant them special seats at His right and left hand in the Kingdom. Matthew's account shows them sending their mother to ask Jesus this favor. On other occasions, the gospels simply say that the disciples argued among themselves "about who was the greatest" (see Mark 9:33–34; Luke 9:46).

Whenever this problem of first-century celebrityism came up, Jesus used one of two sermons. One was a living sermon. He asked a little child to stand beside Him and then said, "Whoever welcomes this little child in my name, welcomes me; . . . for he who is least among you all—he is the greatest" (Luke 9:47–48; see also Mark 9:35–37).

At other times, Jesus simply taught the disciples that they shouldn't act like the rulers of the Gentiles who lorded over those below them. "Instead, whoever wants to become great among you must be your servant, and whoever wants to be first must be your slave—just as the Son of Man did not come to be served, but to serve, and to give his life as a ransom for many" (Matt. 20:26–28).

But even at the Last Supper Jesus knew His disciples still hadn't gotten the message because they were still arguing—about the same thing—who was greatest (see Luke 22:24). That's why He made the greatest demonstration of humility in all Scripture (except for going to the Cross itself). After supper, He got up from the table, girded Himself with a towel, poured water into a basin and began to wash His disciples' feet.

Footwashing sounds strange to us in today's sophisticated culture. Back then, however, Jesus' act had tremendous significance. At first His disciples were horrified. In the ancient Middle East, the feet were considered the filthiest part of the body. Because people usually wore open sandals, the feet were constantly dusty or muddy, depending on the season. When people came into a home, it was customary for a slave to wash their feet after they had removed their sandals at the door.

But when the disciples arrived at the Upper Room for the Last Supper, none of them wanted to play the part of a lowly slave and wash everyone else's feet. To teach them that the way to greatness is through servanthood, Jesus got up and started doing it Himself. Peter protested, "You shall never wash my feet." Jesus answered, "Unless I wash you, you have no part with me" (John 13:8).

Never one to be halfhearted, Peter blurted out, "Not just my feet but my hands and my head as well!" (John 13:9).

When Jesus had finished washing everyone's feet, He sat back down and said, "Do you understand what I have done for you? . . . Now that I, your Lord and Teacher, have washed your feet, you also should wash one another's feet. I have set you an example that you should do as I have done for you" (v. 14).

And then Jesus taught that familiar lesson one more time: "I tell you the truth, no servant is greater than his master, nor is a messenger greater than the one who sent him. Now that you know these things, you will be blessed if you do them" (John 13:16–17).

"Get Off Your Footstool, Dale!"

Today we know "these things," but are we doing them? Whatever celebrityism is, it is not something that empowers people to be humble servants of others. In fact, it is the precise opposite. Celebrityism combines pride and power and becomes insidious and destructive.

Richard Foster believes ". . . the most dangerous people in our media-soaked culture are leaders who believe their own press releases." He remembers going to a large conference where he was given special honors. He was going to be there only twenty-four hours, but the entire time was packed with luncheons, autograph parties and media interviews. By the end of the time, Foster told his wife, "We have to get out of here. I'm beginning to believe all these things people are saying about me."

Foster observes it's strange how we "assume that being on television is some kind of honor. Somehow we feel that television defines who the important people are." He quotes Malcolm Muggeridge, who suggested in *Christ in Media* that if Satan encountered Jesus in the wilderness today, he would add a fourth temptation— namely, to appear on national television![4]

There's one other interesting note on what people of Jesus' day thought about footwashing and the foot itself. If you wanted to insult someone harshly, you kicked him. And the ultimate triumph over your enemy was to make him your footstool.

After I became a Christian, I was sometimes invited by certain speakers to take part in their evangelistic meetings and crusades. I remember working with a young evangelist who hired me to come to New York for meetings in Madison Square Garden. I was appalled at his braggadocio when he said to me he could draw as many people as the "biggest evangelist in the world."

I tried to remind him of the Lord's teaching about taking the low seat at the banquet instead of the high one: Jesus said, ". . . when you are invited, take the lowest place, so that when your host comes, he will say to you, 'Friend, move up to a better place.' Then you will be honored in the presence of all your fellow guests. For everyone who exalts himself will be humbled, and he who humbles himself will be exalted" (Luke 14:10–11).

The young evangelist snapped at me indignantly, "Are you saying I should be sitting on a footstool?"

I told him I was simply quoting the scripture which says the Lord will appoint for us where He wants us to be.

A few years later this same evangelist came to Los Angeles and again invited me to sing a song at one of his meetings. I did, and later he greeted me and said, "That song was great."

"Praise the Lord!" I replied.

He must have remembered our New York encounter because he retorted, "Get off your footstool, Dale!" He still hadn't learned the lesson, and I heard later that his arrogance and lack of self-control had led him into crime and eventually into prison.

Can Humility Help Conquer Celebrityism?

It's not too hard to understand why celebrities, stars and revered leaders have a hard time battling pride and egomania when they are treated like gods. People idolize them by just wanting "to touch them" or speak to them.

Patti MacLeod, whose husband Gavin MacLeod is known to millions as the captain of the "The Love Boat," has had people come up and say, "Hey, may I just touch your husband?" Patti replies, "He's just like you are." But they answer, "Don't say that." People don't want to hear that their stars and idols are "just like they are." They want them to be something better, bigger—larger than life, godlike men and women who can lift them up out of their own dull existence.

Henri Nouwen, who has written many fine devotional books, spent seven months in the Abbey of The Genesee, a Trappist monastery in upstate New York. He recorded his experiences in a book which was later published under the title, *The Genesee Diary*. In one entry he confessed how he had always had a strange desire to be different from other people. And in his monastery surroundings, he was becoming more and more aware how his lifestyle had been influenced by his desire for "stardom." He wrote: "I wanted to say, write or do something 'different' or 'special' that would be noticed and talked about."[5]

Nouwen spoke of becoming increasingly aware of the danger

in making the Word of God sensational. Just as people can be entranced by circus acrobats, they can also be enthralled by preachers who use the Word to draw attention to themselves. Nouwen believes, however, that a sensational preacher might stimulate the senses but leave the spirit untouched. He isn't a way to God. In fact, he gets in the way.

Nouwen was thankful for his monastic experience, which taught him that he couldn't be original. If he had anything to say worth saying, he would find its origin in God's Word. Nouwen recorded in his diary: "What this place is calling me to be is—the same, and *more* of the same . . . the same as Jesus, the same as the Heavenly Father."[6]

I believe wanting to be the same as Jesus is the first step toward humility. Whenever I have tried to act "humble," I have usually wound up being proud of how well I was doing. Scripture teaches us to act justly, love mercy and walk humbly with our God (see Micah 6:8). If we humble ourselves before the Lord, He will lift us up (see Jas. 4:10). And Peter tells us to clothe ourselves with humility toward one another, because "God opposes the proud but gives grace to the humble" (see 1 Pet. 5:5).

Humility is something we do because we are aware of God's presence and His blessing. We should live humbly but not talk about "being humble."

One way the Lord helps me live humility is to give me a "price-tag" experience every now and then. When speaking I often tell of the time Roy was out of town and I was home dressed in what a lot of people refer to as "my grubbies." My hair hadn't been done, I had on no makeup, and the doorbell rang. I went to the door and there stood a tall, good-looking young man. He said, "I would like to see Roy Rogers. Is he here?"

"No," I replied, "I'm sorry but he's out of town. You've missed him."

Then the young man said, "Who are you, the maid?"

"No, not really," I said, wondering if I should enlighten him. But he just went on—"Are you Roy's sister?"

I said, "No."

And finally he said, "His mother?"

"No," I said, "Would you believe his wife?"

He just sort of groaned and said, "Oh, Mrs. Rogers, I'm so sorry—I'm sorry, Dale."

I just said, "I should be the one who is sorry coming to the door looking like this. Don't be sorry. It's not your fault; it's my fault."

It turned out the young man was a gate attendant at a big amusement park in Southern California. As we parted, he wanted to make amends, so he said, "I'll tell you what. I'm on the gate at Magic Mountain and I want you to come out there and bring all your children—free!"

The Lord gave me enough grace to be gracious to the young man, but I have to say it was more than a little deflating to be taken for Roy's mother!

Real Humility Is . . .

But what is real humility? Is it standing around feeling chagrined because you're taken for your husband's mother? Is it being embarrassed when an usher flips the price tag on your new dress out of sight as you sit down in church? These things might help *keep* you humble, but what kind of attitude and lifestyle builds the virtue of humility into your life?

It's much easier to list qualities that are the reverse of humility. We can think of self-centeredness, stubbornness, arrogance, misuse of authority, and any number of others. I like the story about a company commander on a Navy base who confronted a sailor ranked P-4 who refused to clean his room. The P-4 said cleaning rooms was beneath a sailor of his rank. When his commander asked what rank should clean rooms, the sailor said none above a P-3. "You are now a P-3," the commander said, "so go clean your room."[7]

How would the sailor have acted if he had responded to his commander with humility? I think the word we might be looking for is "meekness." In our win-by-intimidation culture, which teaches that "nice guys finish last, so go for the jugular," the word "meekness" creates a picture of Casper Milquetoast trembling while the bully kicks sand in his face at the beach. But the biblical picture of meekness is quite different. The Greek word used for meekness was the happy medium between being too angry or not angry enough.

We are familiar with Jesus' words, "Blessed are the meek, for they shall inherit the earth" (Matt. 5:5). According to William Barclay, one paraphrase of this Beatitude could read: "Blessed is the man who is always angry at the right time and never angry at the wrong time." Barclay goes on to say that this same word was often used to refer to an animal that had been domesticated and trained to obey the words of his master. The "meek" animal was the one who had learned to accept control.[8]

Roy has never broken horses. He always left that to his trainer, Glen Randall. As everyone knows, Roy was extremely fond of Trigger, but he often observed, "Horses are like children. They will get away with whatever mischief they can, particularly in front of a crowd of people."

While Roy was doing a rodeo in St. Louis, he gave Trigger a cue for one of his tricks, but the horse decided to be a smart aleck and not do it. Finally Roy said to the crowd, "You know, sometimes horses can really test your patience. Now Trigger thinks I won't do anything with all of you watching. So if you'll excuse me, I'll have to teach him better." And with that, Roy slapped Trigger smartly with his quirt. And Trigger did the trick immediately. Trigger was meek but he also needed discipline.

To the Greeks, a "meek" person was one who was self-controlled. The Christians simply changed that to say that the meek person is the one who is "completely God-controlled." Meek in the biblical sense is to have the kind of humility that subdues pride.

Another definition of meekness that I like is "teachable." As Barclay says, you can't learn anything if you aren't humble enough to be taught. He refers to Quintilian, the great Roman teacher of oratory, who said of some of his pupils: "They would no doubt be excellent students, if they were not already convinced of their own knowledge."[9] Like every other teacher in history, Quintilian realized it is impossible to teach someone who thinks he knows it all already.

Some Biblical Examples of Meekness

The pages of Scripture are full of illustrations of meekness and what a "meek" person is really like. Saul, the fire-breathing Pharisee, became Paul the apostle who wrote to the Galatians about the fruit of the Spirit, which includes meekness (see Gal. 5:23).

Peter, the blustery, bold fisherman, advised Christian wives that real beauty is found in a "meek and quiet spirit" (1 Pet. 3:4, KJV).

In the Old Testament, Numbers 12:3 refers to Moses as one of the meekest of men, yet he started out in life as a hothead who had to flee after murdering an Egyptian guard in a fit of anger. Moses, leader of an exodus of what some scholars believe were over two million people through the Red Sea and into the wilderness, was anything but a weak, wimpy fellow. Yet the Scriptures call him "meek"—in other words, someone who is always angry at the right time, never angry at the wrong time, someone who is self-controlled—more precisely, God-controlled.

Only once was Moses angry at the wrong time and thus out of God's control. In a fit of impatient pride, he struck the rock at Meribah to show the complaining, faithless Israelites that he could provide water. And for that single act of disobedience he was denied entrance into the Promised Land (see Num. 20: 9–13).

Of course, the supreme example of meekness was Jesus Himself, the most powerful Man Who ever walked the earth, with power to heal and raise the dead. Jesus could have called legions of angels to battle for Him, but instead He meekly went along with those who came to arrest Him in the Garden on the night before He died on the Cross.

Robin Taught Me Humility

In his book, *The Secret of Happiness*, Billy Graham says, "It is not our human nature to be meek. On the contrary, it is our nature to be proud and haughty. That is why the new birth is so essential . . . ."[10]

Billy's words apply so accurately to my own life. I was born anything but meek. I was always headstrong, stubborn, proud, determined to make my own decisions and do things my way. That kind of mindset led to marriage at fourteen and motherhood while I was still a child myself. It led to a second divorce because I was more interested in building my career than I was in my husband. When Christ came in, He started to tame me and gentle me down.

The thing that has taught me humility and meekness more than any other experience was Robin, who was a Down's syndrome baby, the only child born to Roy and myself.

The pregnancy had been difficult. In my second month, I contracted German measles and twice I had to go to bed to prevent a miscarriage. In the seventh month, a blood test showed that I was Rh negative while Roy was Rh positive, not the best match in any situation.

But I wanted this baby and it didn't matter how many problems there were. The difficulties and discomfort would all be worth it when she was born.

Robin Elizabeth Rogers came into the world at seven and one-half pounds on August 26, 1950. The following day, Roy rode as Grand Marshal at a Sheriff's Rodeo and proudly told ninety thousand people he was the father of a new baby girl.

When he got to the hospital that evening, he stopped and looked at Robin before coming to my room. Then he popped in and said, "Honey, she's beautiful; she's got little ears just like yours." We were so happy I couldn't believe it. I was sure there was no way to be any happier, but in just a few days I would be sure there would be no way to suffer any more pain and sadness.

Doctors and nurses noticed something different about Robin almost immediately and started doing tests on her. When they arrived at their conclusion, Art Rush, our manager, learned about it first. They told him Robin was suffering from Down's syndrome (called Mongolism in those days). It's a congenital condition that includes both mental retardation and physical malformation. In Robin's case, she also had a heart condition.

Art later said: "It seemed so cruelly wrong for something like that to be happening to two people like Roy and Dale, people who have worked so hard to help afflicted youngsters in hospitals and orphanages, people who had put their faith in God and lived Christian lives. When I heard the news, it was, without question, the lowest and most desperate moment of my life."[11]

Art called Roy and as they were discussing how to break the news to me, I was already finding it out by accident. The nurse stopped by the room as I was enthusiastically planning our trip home. She wondered—aloud—if the doctors would let me take the baby home. I asked her if there was any reason why I shouldn't. A horrified look seemed to freeze the unbelief on the face of this nurse, who also happened to be a personal friend. With tears in her eyes she asked, "You mean they haven't told you? Call your doctor and demand that he tell you the truth about your baby."

And then she ran out of my room, saying that she had made a terrible mistake in discussing it with me.

When the doctor told me, I wept harder than I had ever wept in my life. The world seemed to have turned totally upside down. What discouraged Roy and me the most is that medical science had found no way to cure or even help Mongolism.

As I cried in my hospital bed, Roy knelt down beside me and said, "Honey, God sent little Robin to us and He'll help us take care of her. We're all going home."

Doctors at the hospital had advised us not to take Robin home but to put her in a facility that cared for Mongoloid children. We just couldn't accept that. We couldn't accept their diagnosis, either. We constantly looked for signs that they could be wrong. We went to specialists, praying that one might give us some hope. Finally, we talked to the head pediatrician at Mayo Clinic in Rochester, Minnesota. We didn't have Robin with us but we showed him a number of photographs of her, hoping he could detect something that would prompt him to want to see her in person. He looked at the pictures only a few seconds and said, "It would be a waste of your time to bring her here . . . . there is nothing I can do to help you."

We thanked him and, as we prepared to leave, he stopped us

and said to Roy, "Mr. Rogers, if I might, I'd like to suggest something. Just go home and love her. She's a special little girl, you know, and she needs your love. I know, because one of our pediatricians has one just like her at home."[12]

We took little Robin into our home to love her and she was, indeed, a special child. I think that all the pain we all went through with Robin helped draw us all closer together. The barriers between me and Roy's daughters, that I had been feeling since we had married three years before, had been slowly coming down. But when Robin arrived they practically crumbled.

When I got home from the hospital with Robin, Cheryl had picked some wildflowers and put them on my bed with a note, "I love you." Little Dusty colored a large picture of Pal, the horse I had been using to shoot movies, and left it on my dressing table. His artwork was inscribed, "To my mother." Linda Lou outlined her hand on a piece of cardboard, sprayed it silver and left it for me as her way of saying "I love you."

But the choicest love offering of all came when Robin was a little over eight months old. Cheryl gave me a Mother's Day card in which she had written these words:

> Thanks a lot for all the things that you've done for me. You've straightened me out on a lot of things I was alone in. And when I needed comforting and experienced advice, you were always there to tell me what I wanted to know. You came to live with us at rather a bad time, with Daddy so sad, and two little girls who were naughty, and a little boy who needed a mother's love that he had never known, and the youngest of those girls had had for only three years. The older girl, when she was smaller, always kept her sorrow and problems in her, and even when you had problems of your own you were always there by our sides and you helped make our Daddy a Christian. I can't find anything fancy to say, but thanks from all of us and we really, really love you.

I kept that card—in fact, I still have it. I looked at it often to gain strength as I tried to cope with having a Down's syndrome baby and knowing that she would probably not grow up to write me any kind of Mother's Day card or anything else.

Our Angel Stayed Less Than Two Years

It's always fascinating to me how God gives us strength to go through certain trials and how He prepares us for those trials, too. Our little girl died of congenital heart failure just two days short of her second birthday. When Robin was born, our pastor, Dr. Jack MacArthur, told me, "This experience will strip all the dross from your life and leave the pure, pure gold." And he was right.

The stress was constant and very wearing. I wanted so badly to talk about Robin, but in those days the public was not ready to accept children with Mongolism. Many people hid Down's syndrome babies in back rooms and talked in whispers about Mongolian idiots. And then there were people, as there are today, who were sure that Robin's condition was due to some sin that Roy or I had committed.

The general public didn't know that Robin had Down's syndrome. All that we had told the newspapers was that she had a heart condition. Roy was the number one box office western star and we had busloads of people coming by the house, just hoping to get a look at our baby.

Robin was a sweet little angel—an angel who came into our home while we were unaware and who stayed for just under two years. There were days when you couldn't tell that Robin was a Down's syndrome child. The next day it was very pronounced.

In the summer of 1952, Cheryl came down with the mumps, and despite all we could do, Robin caught the disease as well. Soon her condition was complicated by encephalitis. By late Saturday, Robin's temperature hit 106. The high fever had reached her brain and she was in tremendous pain. The doctor told us to be prepared for her death. She died the following afternoon when her fever climbed to 108 and she lapsed into a coma.

I was distraught and cried more than I had ever cried in my life. For the first time in our entire marriage, I was of no help to Roy at all. He took care of all the funeral arrangements, and when we arrived at Forest Lawn before the service, I flatly refused to go in with him to look at Robin before the casket was closed for the service.

When Roy came back, his face looked strangely peaceful—more peaceful than it had at any time since Robin had died. He told me, "That was the hardest thing I've ever had to do, Dale, but I'm glad I did. The moment I looked at her, I knew for certain she's with the Lord. She looked like a small, sleeping angel."[13]

"Let Robin Write the Book"

Just a few days after Robin's funeral, I began work on telling the story. I thought to myself, "You have to speak now, you have to testify, because God gave you the strength to go through this even though it was like sitting on a keg of dynamite."

I wrote constantly, trying to do something from my point of view, sharing the hurt that Roy and I had felt inside. But somehow it just wasn't working. One afternoon Roy and I were doing a radio broadcast, and as I was resting away from the mike for a few minutes, I sat down to pray and suddenly heard the Lord saying, "Let Robin write it. Let her speak for herself. You just be the instrument."

That's what I did, and what I wrote became the book, *Angel Unaware*.

When the book was almost finished, doubts assailed me from every direction. I wondered, "Is doing a book like this going to hurt Roy with his fans and the public? Will people misunderstand?"

I didn't care about myself. But I wanted the book to be a witness to the power of Christ and to share with people how we were able to go through our experience with Robin as we trusted Him, knowing He was going to take care of us, whatever happened.

And what about our other children? What about my family and Roy's family? The book would let the whole world know we had had a retarded child—and what would everyone think?

Finally, Roy and I just decided that Christ is more important than any of us, and so we did the book, which had a tremendous ministry. It opened many doors for Down's syndrome children. Back in the 1950s there was practically nothing for children like this. The only school in our area that would even think about taking them was located over a hundred miles from our home and charged one thousand dollars a month.

Having little Robin taught me many things, but the greatest lesson—which I learned completely out of necessity and utter helplessness—was humility. I learned to depend on God completely, and when He took Robin back to Himself, it didn't matter what people thought of me and the book—as long as it accomplished a witness to His power.

Today there is a school in Oklahoma called The Dale Rogers School for the Retarded. In Los Angeles there is The Exceptional Children's Foundation, to which all the royalties for *Angel Unaware* have gone for many years. At first the money went to the American Association for Retarded Children, but that organization disbanded and became The Exceptional Children's Foundation, an agency serving retarded children in the western part of the United States.

Meekness Is God-Given

I believe God teaches all of us meekness. He has taught me the hard way. Losing Robin was only a beginning. We were to lose two other children in tragic circumstances. But through it all I see God working in my life to make me meek—teachable and under His control.

Billy Graham says meekness is not something you can acquire by yourself. You can't get it in college and it can't be mixed in a test tube in some laboratory. Meekness isn't something you inherit—it is God-given![14] As Jesus said: "Take my yoke upon you, and learn of me; for I am meek and lowly in heart: and ye shall find rest unto your souls" (Matt. 11:29, KJV).

If you want to make Jesus your only Star, you have to start by taking His yoke—by being teachable and learning from Him.

What better way to cure celebrityism than to understand what it really means to be a star? Jesus, the only true Star, was born in a stable, laid in a trough used to feed livestock, and grew up a humble carpenter.

If Jesus walked the earth today, would He accept the label *celebrity?* We know that answer before we ask the question. Yet He is the Star of time and eternity. When stars soar into the headlines and across the television screens of the world they are known for a brief time and then they are gone. They are like meteors which shine brightly and then plunge into the earth. But Jesus was a Star Who went into the earth and then rose again to shine forever. He is the only Star worth following.

8

Buy the Truth and
Spend Integrity

We are all born with a bent to look up to role models or heroes whom we want to follow. When I started in radio years ago, my role models were Ethel Waters, Ruth Etting and later, Kate Smith. I tried to sing as they sang, using their voice intonation, phrasing—everything.

As the years passed, though, I discovered there was only one Ethel Waters, one Ruth Etting and one Kate Smith. Dale Evans couldn't be any of those people. She had to be herself. Besides, the more I read articles about my heroes, I became disappointed and disillusioned. They had problems and weaknesses too.

That's the trouble with having heroes. We demand too much of them, hold them up to some kind of an ideal that is really beyond reality. In too many cases, our heroes inevitably let us down.

When news reports came out on Gordon MacDonald and his resignation from InterVarsity due to an extramarital affair, Verne Becker, editor of *University* magazine, recalled that many people had elevated MacDonald to hero status and had been let down hard. They had ". . . hung on his every word and assumed his very presence would trigger massive change or spiritual awakening. We tended to hold him up to nearly impossible standards of perfection."[1]

Several of Becker's friends came to him after hearing the news and wondered, "If *he* can give in to temptation, what hope is there for *me?*" Their assumption implied that Gordon MacDonald was somehow more spiritual, closer to God and better able to stand temptation than others. Those ideas are wrong, of course, because every hero is nothing more than another human being.

The truth is, we can have our heroes and role models, but we must always realize the risk of being disillusioned and dismayed when they finally do fail. When heroes come up smudged with dirt of less than perfect behavior, it's always a good reminder that what we are trying to emulate is their *example*, not their sainthood. A term being thrown around carelessly today is "hero worship." Each time a hero falls, we must learn again that hero worship is wrong. Any time we *worship* a hero, we turn that person into an idol.

What People Are Really Looking For

Why do people keep looking for heroes despite disappointments? I believe they are seeking something that is in short supply in today's society—integrity. The dictionary offers several definitions; one is "in unimpaired or sound condition." The second talks about "strictly adhering to a code," while a third is "the quality or state of being complete or undivided."

You can think of all kinds of synonyms for integrity: true, honest, moral, sound. Ted Engstrom believes that while all these definitions are adequate, they lack flesh and blood. What does integrity look like dressed up in work clothes ready to perform in the everyday world? According to Engstrom, "simply put, integrity is doing what you said you would do."[2]

Engstrom quotes Dr. Lewis Smedes, Professor of Theology and Christian Ethics at Fuller Theological Seminary, who says, "One of the most fundamental acts of society is promise-keeping." We all make promises. Governments and countries make promises to one another. So do companies, friends, business associates and, of course, husbands and wives and parents and children. Every time we make a promise, we are saying, "You can count on me."

So then it's perfectly natural to look for people with integrity. We all want someone we can trust, and we hope our heroes will fill the bill. And yet, we choose role models rather carelessly, or with questionable standards. Jamie Buckingham reported recently that a radio disc jockey polled almost two hundred teenagers in a Jacksonville, Florida, mall. Their top three heroes were: Prince, Madonna and Michael Jackson. When Buckingham polled a group of youth in his local church, the heroes listed were Jesus, Mr. T, Rambo and Spiderman. "Strange company," commented Buckingham, "but at least they listed Jesus first."[3]

Too Many Heroes Are "Non-People"

Adults have a different roster of heroes. Many Christians would name Billy Graham, the President of the United States, a certain congressman or maybe an athlete. Buckingham points out that we usually find our heroes not among people we actually know, but among images, usually projected over television or other media. We don't really know anything about them. All we see is the image that is beamed brightly into our homes each day.

Buckingham writes, "All are non-people who come and go at the flick of a switch." The biblical definition of a hero, says Buckingham, is "a man who stands his ground and does not flee. These are the men and women who consider the odds, make value judgments, and take their stand."[4]

If you are looking for a good biblical hero, Paul the apostle makes a great candidate. He always stood his ground and never fled. In fact, he had to be a role model for people like Peter who had his weak moments even after Christ forgave him that morning on the beach and filled him and the other disciples with the Holy Spirit (see John 20 and Acts 2).

In all his letters, Paul urged Christians to get their eyes off others and keep them on Christ (see especially his advice to Timothy and Titus). As Buckingham says, ". . . a hero never looks around. He just looks ahead . . . . Heroes do what is right because it is right—not because others do it or don't . . . A hero is one who does what his hand finds to do, and lets God control the outcome."[5]

In other words, heroes have integrity.

But where can you find these heroes with integrity? In history books? In the newspapers or on television? What about looking in your church or in your own family? What about your spouse? Your parents? Your children? Or the people who faithfully serve as deacons or deaconesses, Sunday school teachers, year after year? A lot of people make their pastor their hero, but before you make anyone a hero, be sure you *know* that person. Know what he or she really stands for and how he or she lives when the heat is on and there are choices and stands to be made.

My Hero, My Husband

I found my best heroes in my own family. My husband, Roy, has been looked upon as a hero by probably millions of people over the years because of his film image as "King of the Cowboys." But I've known Roy up close and personal for almost forty-five years, and his real-life integrity is as true as the image projected on screen. In fact, more so. Back when I started making pictures with Roy, my father was curious and a bit concerned about this "cowboy actor" I was spending so much time with. Dad wrote me, asking what this Roy Rogers was like.

To put Dad's worries to rest, I sat down to write him about Roy, and part of my letter said:

> He's very plain and humble. In fact, he reminds me a lot of Hillman [my brother]. I've not once seen him trying to upstage another actor in a scene, and no matter what comes up he seems forever to be on the side of the underdog. He does a lot of wonderful things for the people he works with. So no, you don't have to worry. He's a fine person and has become a good friend. The best way to describe Roy Rogers, I guess, is that he rings true.

After Roy and I became Christians, we made a decision always to include a word for God and country in the closing part of our act wherever we might go for personal appearances.

At the 1973 World's Fair, held in Seattle, Roy and I did an act that included some of our children. We closed the very first show with "How Great Thou Art," which we sang from a bridge with the science building behind us. It was a striking scene with all the beautiful turrets and fleecy white clouds above. Ralph Carmichael's Orchestra, as well as additional choral singers, accompanied.

Almost immediately the ABC "hot line" in New York called Art Rush, our manager, with a stinging critique. Art came back from the phone with his eyes drooping lower than Snoopy's ever could. "Dale," he said, "I hate to tell you this, but they said you have to take the name 'Christ' out of the last verse of 'How Great Thou Art.'"

I said, "No way—I will not tamper with that. That's like tampering with 'The Rock of Ages,' and I will not take it out."

We didn't, and we paid the price. Eventually the show was cancelled. Back then it was tough to be an entertainer and talk about Christ or even use His name in a song. Roy and I were among the first entertainers to pioneer efforts to be a positive witness for Christ by declaring our Christian faith. We would always do a patriotic or inspirational number—some kind of hymn to close our show. The network would try to cut out the last two minutes, so no one could hear our inspirational closing, and when that didn't work, we got cancelled. The same thing often happened to Johnny Cash. He told the networks, "You can expect a hymn. If you take me, you've got to take Jesus!"

Roy and I felt the same way; we said the same thing and we, too, got the axe. It's a little better now because the networks have relaxed on this kind of thing, but in the beginning it was tough.

But cancellation didn't really matter, because our relationship to Christ was paramount. For me, being a committed Christian was such a different adventure. I had true joy for the first time because the Eternal Star was shining in my heart and I wasn't about to backtrack or put some kind of bushel over Him.

My Hero, My Son

I came to Christ mainly through the efforts of the other person who has been a true hero for me—my son, Tom. Even when he was a small boy, Tom was a tremendous influence on my life because he was so very real and honest. He was a gifted musician, and when I was working with Republic Studios, I had visions of getting him into the union so he could write musical scores for pictures and possibly get symphony work. I recall Meredith Wilson hearing him play the flute and observing that he had promise for a symphony career.

One day while Tom was still at U.S.C. majoring in music, I came home from the studio and he said, "Frances,* I want to talk with you. Please don't make any more plans for my life. I do not want to be a professional, career musician. I want to reach young people for God through good music."

My mouth flew open and my feathers fell. "Are you telling me you're going to teach?" I asked.

"That's right," he said.

"You'll never make a quarter teaching," I replied.

And then Tom said something I've never forgotten: "There is something in life besides money, and it's what I want."

Obviously, I wasn't a Christian when Tom and I played out that little scene. During those first few months I was married to Roy I had major trouble trying to get his daughters to accept me. It was then that Tom suggested we all go to church. And we did go—to Dr. Jack MacArthur's Fountain Avenue Baptist Church. There I heard a message that reached deep into my soul and convinced me I truly needed to give my life to Christ.

Just a little while after I had accepted the Lord, Tom came to the house and said, "I feel that now I can call you 'Mother' and I want to call Roy 'Dad.' I feel like he is more Dad to me than anyone."

Tom went on to marry Barbara, a fine Christian girl, and they had three daughters, all of whom are strong Christians today. For years he taught music in the public schools and influenced hundreds of youngsters for the Lord. He left teaching to

---

* Because I was so young when Tom was born, my mother took care of him much of the time, until he was almost twelve. He grew up hearing her call me "Frances"—my given name—and he picked it up. Tom called me that rather than "Mom" or "Mother" until right after Roy and I were married.

become minister of music in several churches in southern and central California, but as this book is being prepared for publication, he has applied to return to teaching, hoping for an overseas assignment.

Before I let Christ have my life, I went to church with Tom, heard the sermons and protested under my breath, "You don't understand, preacher. I've got to make it. *Then* I'll turn my life over to Jesus." Tom knew what a struggle I was having and I'm so thankful he was always solid as a rock, even as a teenager. He always took the high road and I believe I followed him because of the tremendous example that he set for me.

Through the years, Roy and I have struggled to be real and human and still, by the grace of God, try to live up to the label of "hero" or "role model" which so many people have put on us. It has been a heavy responsibility, but it always helps to know that none of us is infallible. And every mistake is under the blood of Christ. That's what the cross is all about, but you don't take advantage of it—you don't cut corners or shave the truth.

I've always battled the celebrity image and tried to keep people from idolizing me. I don't pretend to be a star. Whenever possible, I talk with people when they want to talk with me. I don't seclude myself and do my best never to give the impression that I'm special, without problems or flaws.

I like what Bruce Larson said in his book, *Living on the Growing Edge*: "When you show only your virtues, your victories —and by great self-effort exhibit an unflawed image (which is only a half-image)—you mislead people."[6]

In the past, heroes were people who were famous for what they had done—for real accomplishments that mattered. But today heroes are becoming scarce and celebrities are becoming plentiful. Now, as one editorial writer put it, clever P.R. departments enable people to become "famous for being famous." This is true in the Christian ranks as well as in the secular area of life. Perhaps that's why testimonies by "famous believers" get one of two reactions: uncritical awe and admiration or cynical suspicion.[7]

One of the best statements on celebrityism I've seen appears in Daniel Boorstin's book, *The Image or What Happened to the American Dream*. In a chapter on celebrities, he wrote:

> We still try to make our celebrities stand in for the heroes we no longer have, or for those who have been pushed out of our view. We forget that celebrities are known primarily for their well-knownness. And we imitate them as if they were cast in the mold of greatness. Yet the celebrity is usually nothing greater than a more-publicized version of us. In imitating him, in trying to dress like him, talk like him, look like him, think like him, we are simply imitating ourselves.[8]

What Boorstin is really talking about is making celebrities into idols. In a very real sense, engaging in "hero worship" is fooling around with idolatry. And as the psalmist said about idols, "Those who make them will be like them, and so will all who trust in them" (Ps. 135:18). Far better to trust the real Hero, the only Star, Jesus Christ.

Charles Haddon Spurgeon, one of the greatest Bible commentators who ever lived, had this to say about the difference between trusting in the Lord and trusting in men:

> It [trusting God] is better in all ways, for first of all it is wiser: God is infinitely more able to help, and more likely to help, than man, and therefore prudence suggests that we put our confidence in Him above all others.
>
> [Trusting God] is also morally better to do . . . for it is the duty of the creature to trust in the Creator. God has a claim upon His creatures' faith, He deserves to be trusted; and to place our reliance upon another rather than upon Himself, is a direct insult to His faithfulness.
>
> [Trusting God] is better in the sense of safer, since we can never be sure of our ground if we rely upon mortal man, but we are always secure in the hands of our God.
>
> [Trusting God] is better in its effect upon ourselves; to trust in man tends to make us mean, crouching, dependent; but confidence in God elevates, produces a sacred quiet of spirit, and sanctifies the soul.
>
> It is, moreover, much better to trust in God, as far as the result is concerned; for in many cases the human object of our trust fails from want of ability, from want of generosity, from want

of affection, or from want of memory; but the Lord, so far from failing, does for us exceeding abundantly above all that we ask or even think.[9]

How to Have More Integrity

If you want more integrity, begin with putting more trust in Christ. He is the One Who is sound, unimpaired, consistent and Who always does as He has promised. Jesus clearly eclipsed every hero this weary old world has ever known. During His three years of earthly ministry, it was said of Him, "No one ever spoke the way this man does" (John 7:46). Crowds were amazed at Jesus' teaching, ". . . because he taught as one who had authority, and not as their teachers of the law" (Matt. 7:29).

The divine light of His Heavenly Father permeated Jesus' being and words. His detractors were unable to trap Him with their guile and subtlety. He was, is and ever shall be matchless in His stardom! Many Christians are familiar with Jesus' word in John 14:6: "I am the way, the truth, and the life" (KJV). To be committed to Jesus is to be committed to the Truth.

Of course Satan, who specializes in lies and deception, loves it when Christians fall into half-truths and hanky-panky. Another favorite guest I've had on my "Date With Dale" program is Jane Russell, whose stormy film career began with Howard Hughes' "The Outlaw" in the 1940s. Influenced deeply by her godly mother, known throughout southern California for her Bible teaching, Jane never lost her faith in Christ but did go through some very rocky times.

In the preface of her autobiography, *My Paths and My Detours,* Jane tells of becoming a Christian at age six but then getting off track in the glitzy world of Hollywood celebrityism. She likens her detours to ". . . the same long painful journey as that fellow in *Pilgrim's Progress.* Wherever that poor Pilgrim found himself, I've been there twice. And, unlike Pilgrim, I often fell off the path; or, as the Lord said, 'Your detours have been as in a maze.' In those days I can just see Him looking at me sadly and shaking His head."[10]

But Jane has also known the joy of getting back on track

and seeing her Savior smile. In her own salty way, she looks back on what the Lord has saved her from and says: "Satan is the father of liars, and boy, has he tried to hand me a bagful of lies! But, when I listen to that still small voice, I drop that bag and run like hell!"[11]

Jane's graphic words remind me of what King Solomon said about truth and wisdom. Although he wrote thousands of proverbs, one of his most thought-provoking is this: "Buy the truth and do not sell it; get wisdom, discipline and understanding" (ch. 23:23).

Adlai Stevenson once commented on the sorry state of affairs into which this world has fallen by saying, "As scarce as truth is, the supply seems to be greater than the demand." And things have gotten even worse since his death. Much of the world isn't interested in truth, only in results, profits and the bottom line. But Jesus always demanded the truth. He always told those around Him the truth, whether they wanted to hear it or not. Truth is one thing no Christian can do without, for to do without truth is to say that you can do without Christ.

Unfortunately, King Solomon didn't take his own advice. Instead, he bought into lies and sold his birthright for a mess of pottage that included hundreds of wives and concubines, many of whom brought their false gods and religious practices right into the palace in Jerusalem. Solomon had a whole lot to say about getting wisdom and being disciplined, but in the end he lacked the integrity to follow his own teachings.

The One Thing Many Won't Take

Gilbert Beers, senior editor of *Christianity Today*, believes integrity boils down to establishing a system of values and then taking responsibility to live by those values.[12]

I notice that you have to be much more careful about letting anything valuable lie around than you did years ago. Today, anything valuable that is left unguarded will be taken. There is one valuable item, however, that many people won't take, and that is responsibility. It is amazing the lengths to which some people will go to avoid it. As Solomon wrote, "The sluggard is wiser in his own eyes than seven men who can answer sensibly" (Prov. 26:16, NKJB).

Not long ago wire services carried the report of a trial held in Nairobi, Kenya, in which a man being tried was accused of theft. The transcript read as follows:

> *Attorney:* Your Honor, I submit that my client did not break into that house at all. He found the parlor window open, inserted his right arm, and removed a few trifling articles. Now my client's arm is not himself, and I fail to see how you can punish him for an offense committed by only one of his limbs.
> *Judge:* Your argument is very well put. Following it logically, I sentence the prisoner's arm to one year's imprisonment. He can accompany it to prison or not, just as he chooses.
>
> Whereupon the defendant calmly unscrewed his right arm, put it on the table and walked out of court![13]

Failure to take responsibility often destroys the integrity of a marriage. Gavin MacLeod, who has been an outspoken witness since his conversion in 1984, told me that before committing himself to Christ, he was never able to commit completely to a relationship. His first marriage of eighteen years failed and he eventually left his second wife, Patti, because he wanted to get away from the pressures and responsibilities of the marriage.

He said, "I had always been taking care of people all my life. My father died when I was young and I had to take his place. I married young, had children young, went from one marriage into another, and I always had great responsibilities. I guess the enemy got ahold of me. I heard him saying, 'Why do you need this? It's a lot easier on the other side of the fence.' And so I just wanted to get out and experience things—to be a kid without any kind of responsibilities and be as free as the breeze."[14]

How Gavin came back to Patti and to the Lord is recorded in their book, *Back on Course* (with Marie Chapian, published in 1987 by Fleming H. Revell). Today he and Patti do seminars and share the power they have found in Christ to keep a marriage together.

The One Thing Worse Than Sin

It's a short step from not taking responsibility to not admitting sin. Scott Peck, author of the best seller, *The Road Less Traveled*, has said: "The central defect of the evil is not the sin, but the refusal to acknowledge it." In 1983 two United States Congressmen were both censored by the House of Representatives for sexual misconduct. Daniel Crane (R-Ill.) was censored for a 1980 incident with a seventeen-year-old female page. Gerry Studds (D-Mass.) was censored for a 1973 liaison with a seventeen-year-old male page.

That both men deserved censure isn't the issue. It is their respective attitudes that teach something about integrity and taking responsibility. Crane, a dentist from Danville, Illinois, wept when he admitted to his colleagues that he had broken the laws of God and man. He cast a vote for his own censure, facing the House as the Speaker announced the tally.

Studds, a graduate of Yale and a former foreign service officer, made a dramatic speech to the House admitting he was gay and stating that, while he had made a "very serious error in judgment," the relationship with the male page was "mutual and voluntary." He further stated that he had not violated the age of consent in the District of Columbia (sixteen), and that his relationship to the teenager wasn't worth the action or attention the House was giving it. When the roll was taken on Studds' censure, he voted "present" and heard the verdict from the Speaker with his back to the House.

In commenting on these events in the *Chicago Sun Times*, Thomas F. Roeser observed that Studds' actions teach ". . . there is one thing worse than sin. That is denial of sin, which makes forgiveness impossible."[15]

But denial of sin is much in vogue today. In fact, our schools seem to deny that sin even exists. Indeed, children are told to "find the truth within themselves" and make up their own minds about what is right and what is wrong.

In 1987 a book by Professor Alan Bloom, *The Closing of the American Mind*, quietly made the best-seller list because it told the truth about how our colleges and universities are impoverishing the souls of today's students. Bloom's book opens with this chilling sentence: "There is one thing a professor can be absolutely certain of: almost every student entering the university believes, or says he believes, that truth is relative."[16]

Bloom goes on to explain that anyone claiming to have "absolute truth" is looked upon with disbelief, indignation and suspicion. Over the last fifty years, our educators have dedicated themselves to one virtue only—openness. Bloom writes: "Openness—and the relativism that makes it the only plausible stance in the face of various claims to truth and various ways of life and kinds of human beings—is the great insight of our times. The true believer is the real danger."[17]

Bloom is not the only leader ready to speak out about how our educational system has cut our children adrift with no real values and no anchor of moral integrity. In a speech to the National School Boards Association, Secretary of Education William J. Bennett came down hard on what's wrong with the sex education programs in many public schools. Observing that sex education has to do with how men and women should treat one another and themselves, Bennett said, "A sex education course in which issues of right and wrong do not occupy center stage is an evasion and an irresponsibility."[18]

While noting that some teachers do an admirable job, there are too many schools where sex education classes "offer little more than technical information." Students are given no instruction on making moral distinctions. Instead, they are given options of what to do when pregnant and are asked to choose the solutions they like best or least.

Bennett stated that by 1985 an estimated 70 percent of high school seniors had taken sex education courses, but he doubted that such instruction was doing much good. He noted that "more than one-half of American's young people have had sexual intercourse by the time they are seventeen. More than one million teenage girls become pregnant each year. More than four hundred thousand teenage girls now have abortions each year. Forty percent of today's fourteen-year-old girls will become pregnant by the time they are nineteen."[19]

It's no mystery why cheating has become a major scandal in many of the schools in America. A survey taken through a confidential questionnaire given to over two thousand high school seniors in California revealed that 75 percent of them had copied from another student's test paper during an exam, and most of these had done it more than once. Seventy-three percent admitted they had used crib notes to cheat on tests on more than one occasion, and 51 percent confessed to copying word for word from a book and turning it in as their own work.

Nearly 97 percent of the high school seniors said they had seen other students cheating on tests, and 42 percent of the seniors believed that there were some "very good reasons" to cheat. Apparently, the major reason is that they are under pressure to get good grades in high school so they can go on to a good college, and eventually to a high-paying career. Only one percent of the twelfth graders said they would report on a friend whom they saw cheating.[20]

As one high school *honors* student said:

> It's simple. Everybody cheats today. You don't even think about it. The lesson you learn here is that sometimes you have to hit below the belt to get by in life. And then he continued with a shrug of his shoulders, I could never understand why people fail when they have the opportunity to cheat.[21]

Be a *Mensh!*

I don't think it's too hard to find a direct link between cheating on tests to get ahead and putting money, success and celebrityism ahead of everything else in order to be "fulfilled." Our problem, plainly and simply, is that integrity is being sacrificed on the altar of success-happy expediency.

A Yiddish word that describes the person of character and integrity is *mensh*. A mensh is a man or a woman who is honorable and decent and always acts that way. A mensh has hero qualities. He or she is someone to admire or emulate, someone of noble character.

The Jews say, "Now there's a real *mensh!*" Somehow a real mensh conveys a very special sense of respect. Jewish children are often told, "Behave yourself; act like a mensh." There is no more withering comment for one Jew to make about another than to say, "He is not a mensh."

The best thing about being a mensh is that it has nothing to do with material success, wealth (or celebrity status). The key to being a real mensh is character—having a sense of what is right—having responsibility and integrity. In short, menshes are people who buy the truth and never sell it. But they do spend integrity freely, knowing the more they spend, the more they will have.[22]

In these days of plastic celebrities, we need real heroes with integrity. And maybe we need real *menshes* even more!

9

Take a Closer
Walk with Him

One of my favorite hymns, which I have sung many times over the years, is actually an old folk song, the chorus of which says:

> Just a closer walk with Thee,
> Grant it, Jesus, is my plea,
> Daily walking close to Thee,
> Let it be, dear Lord, let it be.

I believe that the closer Christians walk with the only real Star, the less wandering we will do in the bypath meadows of celebrityism. As the second verse of this hymn says, this is, indeed, a world of toil and snares; but if we falter, the Lord is the One Who really cares and Who will always share our burdens.

Where Do You Get Your Direction?

I've heard that there are three kinds of people in the world:

Tradition-directed people look to the past for guidance. Their traditions and practices over the years are what they use for models of behavior.

Other-directed people look around them for clues on how to think and act. Their environment heavily influences them and the peer group is their role model.

    Inner-directed people are guided, however, by their ideals and beliefs that have been implanted deep in their hearts. They have values and they live by them.[1]

Contrary to critics of Christianity who have been having a field day in the wake of all the televangelist scandals, I am not tradition-directed by ancient and dusty codes and regulations. True, I get my information regarding God from an ancient Book, but it contains lasting eternal truths that are as able to change lives today as they were in the first century.

    Our court system in America is based on the principles found in the Ten Commandments. Law school students are required to study them. Truth is truth, no matter what its age might be.

    Nonetheless, evangelicals are often called fundamentalists who refuse to change. Well, they may call me a fundamentalist if they like, but I'm not going to change if it means tossing out the truth. The absolute truth of God in Jesus Christ does not change. When you have no absolute truth which you can trust and follow, you become other-directed, pulled along with every tide and trend. When all truth is relative, you wander in circles, because you have no compass.

    As Ted Koppel, moderator of the popular television show "Night Line," said:

> We have actually convinced ourselves that slogans will save us. Shoot up if you must, but use a clean needle. Enjoy sex whenever and with whomever you wish, but wear a condom. No! The answer is No! Not because it isn't cool or smart or because you might end up in jail or dying in an AIDS ward, but No! because it's wrong . . . in its purest form, truth is not a polite tap on the shoulder. It is a howling reproach. What Moses brought down from Mt. Sinai were not the "Ten Suggestions."[2]

I like Koppel's admonition because it suggests there is an absolute authority behind the Scriptures, and of course that absolute authority is God Himself. As a Christian, I want to be inner-directed—not only by my Christian ideals and values but by the indwelling Holy Spirit of Christ. As we saw in Chapter Six, the Holy Spirit makes His home in each believer (1 Cor. 3:17; 6:19, 20).

In these days of heroes who prove to be all too human and leaders who are as prone to succumb to temptation as the rest of us, we must stay in the Scriptures as never before. I'm not talking about Bible study for the sake of mastering doctrine, as important as that is. But beyond mastering the content of Scripture, we must become better acquainted with the *Christ* of Scripture. We must know Him better and more intimately than ever. We must keep our eyes on Him and Him only—always.

God's Last Word Is Jesus Christ

Some people I have known over the years maintain they see God in nature and prefer communing with Him in beautiful mountain or seashore settings. I, too, see His hand at work in nature, but to know Him best, and even more important, to know Him *personally*, I need to go to His Word. As one scholar put it: "The trees and flowers—with all their messages of God's wisdom —describe nothing of God's saving action in Jesus Christ, His last word (see Heb. 1:1). It is in these Scriptures, *and in them alone*, that we meet God as a person."[3]

Unfortunately, it's all too easy to get our eyes off Jesus, due to fear or to the stresses and storms of life. Peter found that out right after the Lord fed the five thousand. He and the other disciples were sailing their boat back across a stormy Sea of Galilee when, in the fourth watch of the night, Jesus came toward them, walking on the lake. The disciples were terrified and thought they were seeing a ghost, but Jesus called out, "Take courage! It is I. Don't be afraid."

In his typically impulsive way, Peter called back, "Lord, if it's You, tell me to come to You on the water."

Jesus said, "Come," and Matthew's account states: "Then Peter got down out of the boat and walked on the water to Jesus. But when he saw the wind, he was afraid and, beginning to sink, cried out, 'Lord, save me!' (Matt. 14:30).

I like this story because it reminds me of a couple of things:

First, do not go off half-cocked and not count the cost. Second, once I'm out there, walking by faith, I must keep my eyes on the Lord and not let the roaring waves scare me.

There are a lot of roaring waves and storms of controversy right now and every Christian would do well to remember the third great truth of this story. As Peter started to sink, he had sense enough to cry for help and ask the Lord to save him. Peter's experience reminds us that with the Christian, *failure is never final.* Jesus is always there to lend a helping and restoring hand.

Unhealthy Trends in the Hot Tub

Another thing that can so easily get our eyes off Christ and His Word is the glitz and glamor the world has to offer, especially in our materialistic society where narcissism (worship of self) and hedonism (worship of pleasure) are so popular. In his book, *Hot Tub Religion,* J. I. Packer observes that contemporary Christians have again fallen victim to the lures of worldliness. He points to symptoms of "hot tub religion," which find Christians divorcing and remarrying at alarming rates; indulging lax attitudes toward sex and morals; seeking an "overheated supernaturalism" that puts emphasis on signs, wonders, visions, prophecies and miracles; hungering for "soothing syrup from electronic preachers"; and seeking emotional "highs" to go along with "an easy thoughtless acceptance of luxury in everyday living."

"These," concludes Dr. Packer in a rather dry understatement, "are not healthy trends."[4]

Just how unhealthy these attitudes can be is well illustrated by the story of Ananias and Sapphira (Acts 5:1–11), who tried to shortchange their Christian brothers and sisters and then lied about it to Peter's face. That they wound up being carried dead from the assembly is an unforgettable reminder not to take advantage of God's grace.

Celebrityism makes a perfect bedfellow for the three major temptations the world throws at us everyday: the lust of the flesh, the lust of the eyes and the pride of life (see 1 John 2:15–16). I find it interesting that the devil's first temptation to Jesus after forty days in the wilderness was to make bread out of stone. Satan wanted to hit Jesus where it hurt the most—in a very empty stomach. But Christ's rebuttal was, "Man does not live on bread alone." Jesus refuted the devil by saying there is more to life than satisfying the physical appetite. The soul lives on the words that come from the mouth of God (see Matt. 4:1–4).

One Hundred Thirty Days in Solitary for His Bible

Anatoli Shcharansky is a modern example of how important God's Word can be to someone in a hopeless situation. A dissident Soviet Jew, Shcharansky sent his wife out of Russia to freedom in Israel and told her he would follow her soon. But authorities imprisoned him and he spent years in Russian prisons and work camps. The Communists took everything away from him except a miniature copy of the Psalms. Shcharansky refused to give up this bit of God's Word, once spending 130 days in solitary confinement because he would not release the book to the guards.

Twelve years went by and Shcharansky was finally offered freedom. In February 1986 with television cameras rolling, Shcharansky walked away from his Russian guards toward freedom. But in those final moments, the guards thought they'd try one more time to take away Shcharansky's copy of the Psalms. As they wrestled with him, he threw himself face down on the snow. He refused to move an inch without that little book! God's Word had kept him going during his imprisonment and he would not go on to freedom without it.[5]

Anatoli Shcharansky is a twentieth-century cousin to the person who penned Psalm 119. The longest psalm in the psalter, it contains 176 verses of devotion and love for God's law. Here are a few samples of what the psalmist wrote about God's laws, precepts and statutes:

How can a young man keep his way pure? By living according to your word (v. 9).

I have hidden your word in my heart that I might not sin against you (v. 11).

I delight in your decrees; I will not neglect your word (v. 16).

Turn my eyes away from worthless things; renew my life according to your word (v. 37).

May my heart be blameless toward your decrees, that I may not be put to shame (v. 80).

To all perfection I see a limit; but your commands are boundless (v. 96).

Your word is a lamp to my feet and a light for my path (v. 105).

I obey your precepts and your statutes, for all my ways are known to you (v. 168).

Let me live that I may praise you, and may your laws sustain me (v. 175).

What do a Soviet dissident of the '80s and an unknown psalmist who lived anywhere from 1400 B.C. to 500 B.C. have to say to evangelicals at this critical time? What they say to me is they have more love and delight for God's Word than I do—and neither of them has my advantage of knowing Christ personally! The psalmist looked ahead to the Messiah, Shcharansky may still seek His coming, but we know He is here—in our hearts—if we can only remember to look there often to seek His face.

Practice the Presence of God

As Brother Lawrence showed us, we must practice the presence of God, not with three-minute-a-day devotionals or even thirty-minute prayer sessions, but with constant awareness that He is near. Brother Lawrence's given name was Nicholas Herman, and he was born in France in 1611. Nicholas never heard of celebrities or celebrityism. His family was poor, and at age eighteen he met the Lord in what the books call "an experience of conversion." He became a soldier and later a footman.

Not until he was fifty-five did Nicholas enter a Carmelite

monastery and take the name Brother Lawrence. Until his death twenty-five years later, he served in menial roles and is best known for being able to live and walk closely with God in the noisy hospital kitchen where he did everything from peel carrots and potatoes to washing pots and pans.

Although he had little education, Brother Lawrence constantly received letters and personal visits from people who wanted to know "how he did it." They wanted to find the same kind of spiritual reality and confidence that he seemed to experience. Even bishops and church dignitaries turned to him with their problems and doubts.

In his excellent little book, *Closer Than a Brother*, a modern-day paraphrase of *Practicing the Presence of God*, David Winter sums up what Brother Lawrence told everyone:

> Stop putting your trust in human rules, devotional exercises and acts of penance. Instead, exercise a living, obedient faith in God. Live as though He were beside you and with you all the time—*as indeed He is.*
>
> Seek to do what He wants, as and when He commands it, and make His command your joy and chief pleasure. The man who lives like that will be fully human, completely Christian and genuinely happy.[6]

Many fine books and articles have been written on how to have a quiet time. Many of them advocate having a set time for Bible reading and prayer, usually early in the morning each day. As for my own "quiet times," I don't have any specific routine, but I do read Scripture daily and I'm constantly talking with the Lord.

For me, an especially good time to pray is while I'm traveling in my car back and forth to airports, which takes a great deal of time. That's when I often talk to the Lord about anything and everything. Sometimes it's almost embarrassing, but I talk to Him about all kinds of seemingly "inconsequential" things. Of course, nothing is inconsequential to Him; everything we do is His concern, right down to the tiniest detail. He provides for our every need, if we trust Him.

Don't Worry, God Knows about It

Someone who taught me volumes about trusting God came into our lives not long after Robin, our little Down's syndrome baby, was born. We were living in the Hollywood Hills and one day while the girls were playing badminton in the yard, a lady walked by with her daughter. The little girl was about nine or ten years old, wore long skirts and shuffled along in an odd, awkward manner. Linda Lou was friendly to them and later when I got home I invited them over for lemonade and cookies.

The girl's name was Nancy. She had a pretty face that always had a beautiful smile on it. Her mother's name was Marguerite. That first day she showed me Nancy's hands and feet, which were indescribably huge and grotesque. Nancy was the victim of a strange condition she had since birth and, because of her deformities, Marguerite always tried to hide her in the back room. Because she was divorced Marguerite had to work, but she never earned much; and different churches helped the two of them get by.

Before they had moved to southern California, Marguerite and Nancy had lived in San Francisco, and one day an insurance adjustor had come by and seen Nancy, hidden in the back room as usual. When he left, he told Marguerite, "That child is beautiful, don't ever hide her like that again."

That experience gave Marguerite enough courage to stop hiding Nancy and bring her out into the world. And I have thanked the Lord many times that He brought Nancy and her mother into our lives. After Robin was born, I was so despondent that I would occasionally leave her with a nurse and go out to see Marguerite and Nancy in their little home. They were so poor they could have made church mice look like the rich and famous, but Nancy always kept smiling and saying, "Don't worry—God knows what we need." Very often when they had no money at all, a basket of food would appear, given by a church or someone else who knew their need.

Nancy and her mother were such a boost to my spirit. We laughed and talked by the hour. On one visit I spent almost all afternoon with them. I brought them a basket filled with eggs, meat, fruit and other things, and we talked about God's goodness and how He always provides what we need. Before I left for home, I went into the bathroom and, as I turned to leave, an inner voice said clearly: "Leave whatever cash you have." I had exactly thirty dollars in my purse and tucked it under a container of bath powder on the counter.

The next morning Marguerite called and said, "Dale, you don't know what you did. I found the money. All Nancy has ever asked me for is a pair of red shoes. I could never buy her any because of her feet. But we know a cobbler who has told me that he could make her a pair that would fit. And the cost will be thirty dollars. Now Nancy can have her red shoes!"

Little Nancy was one of the greatest inspirations I have ever met. Her condition worsened as she became a teenager and, because her disease caused her to retain a great deal of water, eventually doctors had to amputate both her legs. After the amputations, she and her mother made a trip to Lourdes in France, but not to pray for themselves. Nancy simply wanted to go down into the waters and pray for others that they might be healed.

Nancy outlived Robin by a year or two but she will always live in our hearts. Perhaps more than any other person I ever knew, she helped me understand that God knows all about us and wants to provide for all our needs.

The Little Things Need Attention

We can usually trust God for big problems, but we often think He isn't interested in the mundane things. How wrong that can be. The little things can bring life crashing down if they aren't attended to.

Back in 1982 the news was filled with the tragic destruction of the Ocean Ranger, the world's largest offshore oil exploration platform, which had been erected in the stormy Atlantic 160 miles east of Newfoundland. The Ocean Ranger was gigantic— thirty stories high and built to take eighty-knot winds and thirty-five foot waves. Like the *Titanic*, the ill-fated luxury liner of seventy years before, the Ocean Ranger had been called "indestructible."

One February night a northeaster whipped up and roared down upon the oil platform, but none of the eighty-four crew members was alarmed. Ocean Ranger had taken far worse storms than this with no problems and they felt secure. It was no wonder then that when an exceptionally large wave crashed into the rig and broke a window in the control room, no one was particularly concerned. What went unnoticed, however, was one tiny detail. Water short-circuited a tiny switch which caused one of the valves in the platform's giant peer-like stilts to open and allow the sea to pour in.

By the time the short-circuited switch was discovered, the Ranger was listing badly as waves of more than sixty feet pounded against it. Rescue was attempted, but to no avail, and all eighty-four crew members perished—because no one noticed that one little detail—the tiny switch that had short-circuited.[7]

We Are Too Busy to Beware

How can we possibly bring the tiny details of our lives to God when we have so many major details and important bases to cover all day long? Our besetting problem, of course, is that we are too busy. As David Winter says, "The modern world makes it harder and harder to live a 'spiritual' life."[8] We are surrounded by dehumanizing machines, gadgets, processes, technologies of every kind. Winter says computers are replacing minds and psychotherapy is replacing prayer.

While I can't prove it, I've got a hunch our left brain—the side that is rational, cool and calculating—is growing larger than our right—the side that is warm, creative and playful. We roar into each day's schedules, ignoring signs or desk placards like "Beware of the Barrenness of a Busy Life." We dash around like Martha and wonder why Jesus isn't more concerned that we have to do all this work.

But Jesus' answer to us is the same one He gave Martha: "Martha, my dear, you are worried and bothered about providing so many things. Only a few things are really needed, perhaps only one. Mary has chosen the best part and you must not tear it away from her!" (Luke 10:41–42, Phillips).

No matter how busy we get, we must join Mary in making sure we always get some of "the better portion"—time with the Lord Himself. We need those quiet moments when we can put our roots down deep into the Lord's love and wisdom. An unknown poet put it like this:

> Nothing that happens can hurt me,
> Whether I lose or win.
> Though life may be changed on the surface,
> I do my main living within.[9]

Susannah Wesley bore nineteen children, among them the great eighteenth-century evangelist, John Wesley. You can imagine what some of her days must have been like! But when Susannah wanted to pray and meditate, she always used the same approach. She sat in her rocker and covered her face with an apron. Her children knew this was Mother's "quiet time" and she was not to be disturbed![10]

In his devotional book *Abundant Living*, E. Stanley Jones speaks of our need for "islands of solitude," where we can meditate and have time with the Lord. Without these islands of solitude to which we can flee, our days become as impoverished as this tongue-in-cheek description of how one "busy man" lived out his life:

> And wow he died as wow he lived,
> Going whop to the office and blooie home to sleep,
> Biff got married and bam had children and oof got
>   fired.
> Zowie did he live and zowie did he die.[11]

Sometimes God Brings Us Up Short

Sometimes when we start rushing around too fast, God brings us up short to remind us that we should slow down a bit.

I love the story by Lloyd Ogilvie, who had made plans to attend a formal dinner. He had a busy agenda that day and got back home with almost no time to get dressed. Frantically, he threw on his tux pants and tux shirt and reached into the closet for what he thought was his tux coat. As he walked into the grand affair, somebody came up and said, "Oh, a blazer with your tux?"

Lloyd, a fastidious dresser, was chagrined to say the least, but he just laughed about it. He couldn't go home and change because there wasn't time. And I believe he even had to speak that night as well.

I heard Lloyd tell that story on himself, and his point was that sometimes, when we become a little inflated or important and too busy, God allows little things to happen to sort of cut us down to size. He said, "It was a very good thing to have happen. I think it was the Lord's way of making me slow down."

As I was completing work on the manuscript for this book, I got my own "slow down" message from the Lord. In my case, however, He jerked a little harder on the reins. At an annual physical, I mentioned to the doctor that I had been feeling "funny little flutterings in my chest." He put me on a treadmill and, after one and a half minutes, he had all the information he wanted. I had tachycardia, which means the heart changes rhythm without warning. He also did some further tests that revealed I had very high cholesterol and triglyceride readings. My blood pressure (204/90) didn't please him very much either.

"Mrs. Rogers," he said, "you have hypertension and *must slow down*. You should cut out the coffee, go on a diet and start walking regularly for exercise."

And so I have. Quitting coffee was hard! I had no idea how hooked I was. But walking is enjoyable; it gives me more time to pray and talk things over with the Lord. One thing we talk about is how I can cut down on my activities and learn when to say yes and when to say no. The no's are harder, especially when invitations to speak come in.

I've always had tremendous energy, but now that energy needs bottling, and I'm my own worst enemy. I have to do more than say, "Yes, the doctor's right. I really ought to slow down and take it easier." If it doesn't go any further than that, I won't change some bad habits I've developed. And I'm learning that I should spend even more time listening to the Lord's wisdom for my life. It's so easy to lose sight of that in the noise and din of daily living. I've got to remember that Elijah didn't find the Lord in the windstorm, the earthquake or the fire. He finally heard the *still, small voice* saying, "Why are you here, Elijah?"

Then and only then could Elijah share his heart and his troubles and get instructions about what to do next (see 1 Kings 19:11–18). As the Lord said through the pen of the psalmist, "Be still, and know that I am God; I will be exalted among the nations, I will be exalted in the earth" (Ps. 46:10).

What I have to learn is to "be still." Most Christians I talk with are usually interested in getting closer to God. We all want more intimacy but it's hard to develop. As one writer on spiritual intimacy said, "Intimacy progresses gradually: the more we see of the Lord's glory and grace, the more we want to know Him. The more we give ourselves to Him, the more we want to give. The more we become one with Him, the more we long for a deeper oneness."[12] She goes on to say that we must again go to the psalmist for instructions: "Taste and see that the Lord is good" (ch. 34:8). Blessed is anyone who takes refuge in the Lord. As we have one taste of Him, we want more and more—until our appetite is insatiable.

To taste of the Lord, we must know where to shop. A friend sent me the following allegory. The author is unknown, but what he or she writes about can be known by every Christian:

HEAVEN'S GROCERY STORE

I was walking down life's highway a long time ago. One day I saw a sign that read, "Heaven's Grocery Store." As I got a little closer the door came open wide, and when I came to myself, I was standing inside. I saw a host of angels; they were standing everywhere. One handed me a basket and said, "My child, shop with care." Everything a Christian needed was in that grocery store; and all you couldn't carry, you could come back for more.

First I got some Patience; Love was in the same row; farther down was Understanding—you need that everywhere you go. I got a box of Wisdom, a bag or two of Faith. I just couldn't miss the Holy Spirit, for it was all over the place. I stopped to get some Strength and Courage to help me run the race. By then my basket was getting full, but I remembered I needed some Grace. I didn't forget Salvation, for Salvation was free. So I tried to get enough of that to save both you and me.

Then I started to the counter to pay my grocery bill, for I thought I had everything I needed to do my Master's will. When I went up the aisle I saw Prayer and I just had to put that in. For I knew when I stepped outside I would run right into sin.

Peace and Joy were plentiful. They were on the last shelf. Songs of Praises were hanging near, so I just helped myself. Then I said to the angel, "Now, how much do I owe?" He just smiled and said, "Just take them everywhere you go."

Again I smiled at him and said, "How much do I really owe?" He smiled again and said, "My child, Jesus paid your bill a long time ago."

10

Serve the Star,
Not the Image

One of the greatest dangers in celebrityism is its power to infect millions of people with what I call "ordinaryitis." Someone with a good case of this prevalent disease can usually be heard saying: "What can I do about all these problems? I'm just an *ordinary* person."

Chuck Colson believes that we have been conditioned to think the only way to work on any problem is through the government or through someone famous who has some clout and who would be heard by an otherwise indifferent world. According to Colson:

> This political/celebrity illusion has become the dominant myth of our times. And few have embraced it with more enthusiasm than the Christian community. We seem to think we need a big parachurch organization or a well-known celebrity in order to accomplish anything for the kingdom of God. As a result, the church has elevated popular pastors, ministry leaders and televangelists to the dubious pedestal of fame—only to watch many topple in the winds of power, influence, and adulation. All the while, "ordinary" Christians feel more and more frustrated.[1]

Who Wants to Be Just "Ordinary"?

Christians should know better than to buy into the myth of "ordinaryitis," but they do, nonetheless. Why? In his book, *Whatever Happened to Ordinary Christians?*, Jim Smoke says:

In the age of the sensational, the superb, and the extraordinary, who in his right mind wants to be ordinary? Ordinary is vanilla when everyone wants pistachio. Ordinary is plain wrap when everyone wants fancy. Ordinary is average when everyone wants to be above average. Ordinary is being in the line when everyone wants to be at the head of the line. Ordinary is not attracting attention when everyone wants attention. Ordinary is simply not IN.[2]

The apostle Paul, however, was always glad to settle for ordinary Christians. He wrote to the Corinthians, who were totally confused and carnal because they kept running around looking for extraordinary signs, wonders and experiences: "Brothers, think of what you were when you were called. Not many of you were wise by human standards; not many were influential; not many were of noble birth. But God chose the foolish things of the world to shame the wise; God chose the weak things of the world to shame the strong . . . so that no one can boast before him" (1 Cor. 1:26-27, 29).

It's my hunch that God is looking for more ordinary Christians who will stand up and praise Him instead of boasting about themselves or somebody they think is really great. We have one Star and He is enough. He is Jesus, the Star of all time and eternity. But Jesus never came on like power-money-sex-hungry rock stars who get interviewed on talk shows by seemingly awe-struck hosts. He never acted or talked like a "great world leader." In fact, He turned the world's standards of stardom and "great-ness" upside down. He told us that if we want to be big or great, we have to be little and least. We must serve, not be served or adored and worshiped.

Moody and Machen: Humble Servants

We have already seen how and why Jesus washed the feet of
the disciples to model humble servanthood (Chapter Seven). Stories of how Christians have followed the Lord's example over the
centuries are hard to come by, especially in recent years. But I have
found two from the lives of great servants of the past—Dwight L.
Moody and J. Gresham Machen.

Dwight L. Moody, the great evangelist of the late nineteenth
century, invited several English preachers to attend a conference
at Moody Bible Institute. Before retiring, he walked the halls to
check on things, and rounding a corner he came upon the guest
rooms where the English pastors were staying. Neatly placed outside each door was a pair of shoes that were in need of polishing.

Because Moody had been to England, he knew of the practice there to have guests place their shoes outside the door upon
retiring to allow the host to polish them before morning.

Several students happened by and Moody said, "These ministers are following the custom of their country where they always
put their shoes out to be cleaned at night. Would you fellows get a
piece of chalk from a classroom, put the numbers of the rooms on
the soles of the shoes, then shine them nicely?"

But one student protested and said, "Mr. Moody, I didn't
come to this institution to clean shoes. I came here to study for
the ministry." All his companions agreed, but Moody did not
lecture or admonish them in any way. He simply said, "Very well,
you may go back to your rooms."

Then Dwight L. Moody collected all the shoes, took them to
his own room, polished them until they shone and put them back
in place by each door.

Dr. J. Gresham Machen was one of the theological giants of
the early twentieth century. During World War I he applied for
service with the overseas Y.M.C.A. In France he was assigned the
job of manufacturing and selling hot chocolate drinks in a canteen for servicemen. In those days instant hot chocolate was not
available. Machen had to rise very early in the morning, reduce
huge bars of sweet chocolate into shavings, add water and then

bring the giant pot to a boil. Later he added condensed milk and boiled the concoction some more. By 7:00 A.M., he was ready to open the canteen for customers. He never got his own breakfast until well after 9:00 o'clock.

One of the great Christian scholars in all history, Machen, who was an ordained professor at the time, would have liked heavier, more "meaningful" responsibility, but he was content to serve in even that menial way.[3]

After the war, Machen went on to write books like *Christianity and Liberalism*, which in many ways is a statement against the worldly values that have spawned celebrityism in our times. In his defense of biblical Christianity, Machen said Christians ultimately put their hope in heaven. He wrote: "[Christianity] views this world under the aspect of eternity; the fashion of this world passes away, and all must stand before the judgment seat of Christ."

At the opposite end of the spectrum was—and still is—the modern liberal church which accepts only the social teachings of Jesus but not His deity, resurrection or atoning death for sins. According to Machen, for the liberal, ". . . heaven has little place, and this world is really all in all . . . this world is really the center of all his thoughts."[4]

Celebrityism Centers on This Life

Today we see in so many ways that celebrityism, even Christian celebrityism, emphasizes this earthly life, getting goodies and fame and notoriety here and now, rather than serving God and receiving a heavenly reward.

Jesus' concept of becoming a servant in order to be great is light years away from the proud evangelist who told me he would never settle for "sitting on a footstool." It is also a far cry from the stand taken by Jimmy Swaggart, who defied his church and refused to stay out of the pulpit for a year, as any other fellow minister in the Assemblies of God would have been asked to do.

Instead of obedient servanthood, a year of repentance and quite likely serious financial problems for this TV ministry, Swaggart opted for forcing the Assembly of God officials to defrock

him and going back into the pulpit—and on the TV airwaves—
in an effort to keep millions of dollars flowing in. He can claim he
is "doing it all for Jesus," but the world—Christians and pagans
alike—watches and knows better.

If we look to Jim Bakker for examples of footwashing and
servanthood, we are equally disappointed. One story, reported in
Time magazine, quotes former trusted anonymous aides of Bakker
who said on one occasion Jim called a staff meeting in his luxuri-
ous dressing room after a regular weekday PTL show. He removed
his shoes and socks, put his feet up, and requested that someone
rub them. One PTL vice-president came forward to comply with
what another witness called a "humiliating request."[5]

What actually happened and what was really said is hard to
say. Stories have a way of being slanted or repeated inaccurately.
Everyone present in this meeting would have his own view, but
wouldn't it have been encouraging to hear a story like this and
have Jim Bakker doing the foot rub?

But instead of bewailing the self-serving failure of fallen leaders, we need to look to our own responsibility to be servants. I want
to be an ordinary Christian, doing what my hands find to do for
Christ. Instead of tiptoeing around, apologizing for my faith because some highly visible folk have had problems, I prefer to let my
life and actions speak for the Lord. Every time I go out to speak, my
prayer is the same: "Lord, send Your Spirit to speak through me.
Help me not to try to 'perform' but simply to be used."

Christ's Greatest Act of Servanthood

The essence of celebrityism is to say in your heart, "I want to
be like so-and-so" (just name your favorite star or celebrity). The
essence of Christian servanthood is to say, "I want to be like
Christ." I've often seen the quote, "He became like us that we
might be made like unto Him." Jesus' supreme act of servanthood
was not healing the sick, feeding the five thousand, turning the
water into wine or even washing feet. His greatest demonstration
of service was dying on the cross for your sins and mine. Matthew

and Mark both record Jesus' words "the Son of Man did not come to be served, but to serve, and to give His life as a ransom for many" (ch. 20:28; ch. 10:45).

In his wonderful book, *The Cross of Christ*, Dr. John Stott explains that Christians serve Christ only because He first completed His service to us " . . . by laying down His life as a ransom . . . . it was only by serving that He would be served, only by suffering He would enter into His glory."[6]

Stott goes on to say that it seems to be "definitely beyond doubt" that Jesus knew Isaiah 53 was all about His substitutionary death. This famous chapter from Isaiah's prophecy speaks of how Jesus was despised and rejected, that He was a Man of sorrows and acquainted with grief, that He was stricken, smitten and afflicted. But the verses we remember most are these:

> . . . He was pierced for our transgressions, he was crushed for our iniquities; the punishment that brought us peace was upon him, and by his wounds we are healed. We all, like sheep, have gone astray, each of us has turned to his own way; and the Lord has laid on him the iniquity of us all (Isa. 53:5-6).

Later in this same chapter, Isaiah adds:

> Yet it was the Lord's will to crush him and cause him to suffer, and though the Lord makes his life a guilt offering, he will see his offspring and prolong his days, and the will of the Lord will prosper in his hand. After the suffering of his soul, he will see the light of life and be satisfied; by his knowledge my righteous servant will justify many, and he will bear their iniquities (Isa. 53:10-11).

As the righteous Servant, Christ the sinless One, was made ". . . to be sin for us, so that in him we might become the righteousness of God" (2 Cor. 5:21). To serve Christ, we must be like Him, but how? There are no cut and dried rules. To be like Christ we need to be of one mind and one spirit with Him. We must study the qualities of His life and apply these to every situation we face each day.

Qualities of Christlikeness

We need right beliefs about Jesus, but we need the fruit of His Spirit even more. Following is a list of qualities of Christlikeness. They all sound very ordinary, except it takes extraordinary strength to develop them—strength that comes from the Lord and no one else.

Non-retaliation: ". . . Christ suffered for you, leaving you an example . . . when they hurled their insults at him, he did not retaliate; when he suffered, he made no threats. Instead he entrusted himself to him who judges justly" (1 Pet. 2:21–23).

Menial serving: "Now that I, your Lord and Teacher, have washed your feet, you also should wash one another's feet" (John 13:14).

Humility: "Your attitude should be the same as that of Christ Jesus: Who . . . made himself nothing, taking the very nature of a servant . . . and being found in appearance as a man, he humbled himself and became obedient to death—even death on a cross!" (Phil. 2:5–8).

Gentleness: "Take my yoke upon you and learn from me, for I am gentle and humble in heart, and you will find rest for your souls" (Matt. 11:29).

Self-denial: "If anyone would come after me, he must deny himself and take up his cross and follow me" (Matt. 16:24).

Patience under trial: "It is better, if it is God's will, to suffer for doing good than for doing evil" (1 Pet. 3:17). "Let us fix our eyes on Jesus, the author and perfecter of our faith, who for the joy set before him endured the cross, scorning its shame, and sat down at the right hand of the throne of God" (Heb. 12:2).

Forgiving: "Bear with each other and forgive whatever grievances you may have against one another. Forgive as the Lord forgave you. . . . I tell you, not seven times, but seventy-seven times" (Col. 3:13, Matt. 18:22).

Acceptant: "Accept one another, then, just as Christ accepted you, in order to bring praise to God" (Rom. 15:7).

Joyful: "If you obey my commands, you will remain in my love, just as I have obeyed my Father's commands and remain in his love. I have told you this so that my joy may be in you and that your joy may be complete" (John 15:10–11).

Obedient: "But if anyone obeys his word, God's love is truly made complete in him. This is how we know we are in him: Whoever claims to live in him must walk as Jesus did" (1 John 2:5–6).

Loving: "This is how we know what love is: Jesus Christ laid down his life for us. And we ought to lay down our lives for our brothers" (1 John 3:16).[7]

In the above list, love is last. But instead of being least, it is the sum of all the other qualities of Christlikeness. Loving doesn't mean feeling, although feelings are part of loving. Loving means acting, doing something to serve and care for others. An act of love always includes some sort of self-denial. In effect Jesus asks all of us, "Do you want to love as I loved? Then deny yourself, take up your cross and follow me" (see Mark 8:34).

To Take Up Your Cross, Deny Yourself

There are many opinions on what Jesus meant by "bearing one's cross." John Stott says the Christian's cross is not a crabby spouse, an overbearing boss, an illness or some other impediment or burden. The cross ". . . is instead the symbol of death to the self."[8] Self-denial doesn't mean swearing off cigarettes, dessert or too much TV. All those disciplines could be involved, but at the heart of self-denial is ". . . actually denying or disowning ourselves, renouncing our supposed right to go our own way."[9]

But self-denial is only one part of loving servanthood. The other part is self-affirmation, which is a much more accurate term than "self-love." As we saw in Chapter Six, we should never doubt our self-worth because we belong to Christ, Who gave His life to ransom us and pay the penalty for our sins. As Stott says, "Nothing indicates more clearly the great value Jesus placed on people than His determination to suffer and die for them."[10]

If we are committed to curing celebrityism by making what Jon Johnston calls a "radical reassessment of human worth" (see Chapter One), the place to start is at the cross. Stott writes: "It is only when we look at the Cross that we see the true worth of human beings. As William Temple expressed it, 'My worth is what I am worth to God; and that is a marvelous great deal, for Christ died for me.'"[11]

In Ephesians 4:22-24, Paul describes what could be called the Christian's split personality: "You were taught, with regard to your former way of life, to put off your old self, which is being corrupted by its deceitful desires; to be made new in the attitude of your minds; and to put on the new self, created to be like God in true righteousness and holiness."

Gavin and Patti MacLeod know firsthand the price actors must pay when they put on the "new self." Since they both came to Christ several years ago, they have turned down a lot of "opportunities" that could drag them back into the old way of life.

Gavin told me recently: "Just last week we turned down an enormous opportunity. We had been praying to the Lord that morning and asking Him if He would please send some money our way because we really happened to need it at the moment. Later that day my agent called from New York with an offer of a prestigious part in a musical in Atlantic City. The problem was that it featured and glorified sin. I called our pastor, Jack Hayford, to talk it over because I felt we just couldn't do it. He gave us great advice: 'You're being tempted because you need the money, just as Jesus was tempted in the wilderness.'

"So we turned it down, and wouldn't you know that just a little while later somebody visited from New York, where they're doing some new theatre, and he offered me the same part in the very same musical! The devil just doesn't give up."

Gavin and Patti understand that taking up the Cross to follow Christ means denying yourself in practical ways. When you deny yourself, you say *no* to the old self. When you affirm and accept yourself, you say *yes* to the new self Christ has redeemed.

Scripture teaches us in innumerable places that putting on the new self means doing our duty—serving as Jesus served. One theology professor believes twentieth-century evangelicalism has been guilty all too often of the heresy of "Boy Scout Christianity," which has ". . . truncated the Christian Gospel to a half-Christ (Savior, but not Lord) and a half-salvation (blessings but not duties)."[12]

I believe the heresy of celebrityism has done the same thing by putting too much emphasis on glamour, glitz and "exciting feelings." The Bible doesn't have much to say about Christians *feeling* good, but joy, fulfillment and blessing are always a byproduct or result of *doing* good. After we are saved by grace, the Lord gives us His marching orders: "For we are God's workmanship, created in Christ Jesus to good works, which God prepared in advance for us to do" (Eph. 2:10).

Sometimes we are duped into thinking that "duty" is a drag, something bad we must do before we can enjoy ourselves. But our duty is assigned personally by God and nothing is hidden from His eyes. Servanthood isn't an option we can take or leave according to how we feel. Servanthood is what following the only Star is all about.

Carol Lawrence Became a Willing Servant

Carol Lawrence, the lovely, talented actress and singer, has shared with me how coming to Christ and becoming His willing servant has transformed her life. In the late 1970s, when her two sons were still quite young, she suffered three terrible blows right in a row: the disintegration of her marriage to Robert Goulet, the death of her father of cancer and, six months later, the death of her mother of heart disease.

Carol and Robert tried for reconciliation, but unfortunately it was unsuccessful, and a long and tedious court battle for settlement and proper child visitation rights ensued. In the midst of all this chaos, Carol kept trying to perform and, while on stage, she managed quite well. But later, in the quiet of her home, depression and despair crushed her under a terrible weight until she wept uncontrollably.

Carol recalls how it all became too much: "One night I started to sob so violently that I couldn't breathe. I was like a small child crying itself into exhaustion. And I got down on my knees and said, 'Jesus, You promised us that You would never give us a burden we couldn't bear, and I am drowning in this one. I have to hand it over to You or I'm going to die.'"

When Carol came to Christ, in the quiet of her home, "It was as if a rock had been lifted off my heart. For the first time I could stop crying and I knew for certain that I never had to be alone again."

Since that time Carol has been Christ's committed servant, continually trying to give testimony to the healing in her life and gaining the spiritual nourishment that comes through sharing the greatest message on earth. She began hosting telethons for children, ". . . to try to give back some of the blessings the Lord had given me. I discovered that as I served Him and gave Him the glory and honor He deserves, He opened doors and windows I would never have had a chance at otherwise."

While working on telethons, Carol met a young composer from Bel Air Presbyterian Church, where she had been attending and receiving love and spiritual support. Ron Harris sang one of his songs during a church service, a song that Carol thought would be perfect for a children's telethon. She introduced herself, learned the song, and not only sang it on telethons but on the Johnny Carson Show as well.

As a result of the Carson Show, Word Records called her and asked her to record. Later, Word wanted her to do religious concerts to promote the albums, and out of those Ron Harris composed a lovely one-woman show focusing on the life of Mary, mother of Jesus, which Carol presented all over the United States and Canada. She did the life of Mary—from the annunciation to the crucifixion—at the Crystal Cathedral, and that in turn led to an opportunity to play Mary in Crystal Cathedral presentations of "The Glory of Christmas" and "The Glory of Easter."

"The Glory of Easter" 1988 production was a highlight for Carol. For over a month, twice a night for five nights a week, she portrayed Mary at the cross, which includes a moving scene where the players reproduce Michelangelo's "Pieta," the sculpture showing Christ in the arms of His mother.

Carol recalls: "In this scene, they took Christ down from the cross, put Him in my arms, and I sang a special song that Ron Harris had written, 'This They Cannot Take from Me.' It was one of the most moving and draining things I have ever done in my life. I literally sobbed through each production and could hear people sobbing in the audiences as well."

Carol believes the song had such great power because everyone in the cast sought to glorify Christ completely. She prayed, "Lord, I will do it according to Your plan, because I'm not the celebrity. I'm not the star of this production; *You* are."

Carol looks back over her past years of serving her Lord and says: "From the moment I turned my burdens over to Christ and gave Him full control of my life, He has kept weaving a beautiful tapestry. When you are able to stand up and give your testimony, the Lord enriches your life. He enriches your career and, above all, He enriches the channel you become for His love."

Carol's story is a lovely example of what happens when a life is given to Christ and He is allowed to fill it with service and blessing. Carol's example reminds us to ask ourselves how we rate as servants. Here are four questions that are well worth pondering:

Do I truly love Christ as my Lord and Master?

Do I serve Christ with real joy?

Am I faithful in doing my duty?

Am I content with the lower seat (the footstool) and the lower profile?

A conductor of a great symphony orchestra was once asked to name what he thought was the most difficult instrument to play. The conductor reflected for only a moment and then said, "Second fiddle. I can get plenty of first violinists, but to find one who can play second fiddle with enthusiasm—that's a problem."[13]

Christ's servants should be able to play second fiddle with no problem. In fact, they should never notice *what* fiddle they play because they have their eyes on the Master Conductor—the Star of the symphony. They are too busy taking His directions to worry about who is getting first billing or celebrity status.

The Only Real Star Shines on Forever

We opened this look at celebrityism with a story by Chuck Colson, who discovered how very cold it can be for Christians out on the book tour trail. At about the time the televangelist scandals were breaking, Colson felt the sting of snide derision heaped on "God's little goof-balls" by a Dallas talk show host. And the bashing was meant for all Christians, not just the Bakkers.

A few days later Chuck went to a little town in Delaware to break ground for a prison chapel and to hold a dedication service sponsored by his Prison Fellowship organization. The town's dignitaries, and even the Lieutenant Governor, were present. Several people, including Colson, made remarks before turning over shovels full of black soil. The chapel, planned to seat 275, would stand in the center of the prison yard surrounded by cell blocks and razor wire. Colson thought of the miracle he was taking part in: "A church, planted in the middle of humanity's hell on earth."

Everyone later adjourned to a nearby Methodist church for supper and an evening service. The sumptuous meal of roast turkey, crisp home-grown vegetables, hot baked buns and home-made pumpkin ice cream was served by Mennonite farm families. Colson notes that he had attended White House state dinners that could not top such a feast.

Finally everyone crowded into the sanctuary with its old oak pews to celebrate a Prison Fellowship community service project. Their special program had allowed five prisoners to be furloughed to the care of Christian host families where they had worked for two weeks restoring a senior citizens' center and a home for an elderly retired couple.

Delaware's Commissioner of Corrections sat wide-eyed as the five prisoners spoke about their experiences during that work furlough. They choked up with emotion—something they wouldn't dare do back in prison—as they talked about how much it had meant to live with Christian families and accomplish something useful while growing in their faith.

To close the service, the chaplain asked each host family to stand at the altar with their inmate. They all lined up in front of the congregation, and one little blonde girl of six or seven took the hand of the prisoner who had lived in her home. As the concluding prayer was given, she never took her eyes off of his. Colson writes:

> His eyes were misty. So were mine. I needed to be in Georgetown for that simple Sunday service; it put my book tour experiences into perspective. Yes, there is a wide gulf between Dallas and Delaware, between the image and the reality of Christianity. It is a gulf so wide, in fact, that maybe it can't be closed. But does that really matter so much after all? The image may reign, but beyond the caricatures of television and radio stations, the reality lives on.[14]

I expect some harsh criticism in some circles for writing this book, but I don't mind. I really don't, because I don't count—God counts. We all have to think, pray and do something about this—whether we're minister, missionary or lay person. In the minds of some, the Christian image has become a twisted caricature. But I know there is hope. As someone said, "Hope is not pretending that troubles don't exist. . . . It is the trust that they will not last forever, that hurts will be healed and difficulties overcome. . . . It is faith that a source of strength and renewal lies within to lead us through the dark into the sunshine of His love."[15]

All we do and believe is based on the hope we have in Jesus Christ. Whatever the image, it doesn't matter. The reality will always live on, as the only real Star shines in the darkness—and in our hearts.

Notes

1. Only One Star—Only One Hope

1. Chuck Colson, "Reflections on a Book Tour: It's Cold Out There," *Jubilee*, The Monthly Newsletter of Prison Fellowship, February 1988, p. 7.
2. By Phil Boutelje and Harry Tobias. © 1950, 1951 Tobey Music Corp. (Renewed) Controlled in the USA by Chappell & Co. and Harry Tobias Music. All Rights Reserved. Used By Permission.
3. See Dr. Tim LaHaye, *Capital Report Newsletter*, March 1988, p. 5.
4. David Aikman, "The Press is Missing the Scoop of the Century," *Christianity Today*, March 4, 1988, p. 12.
5. Aikman, p. 12.
6. Philip Yancey, "Jim Bakker Made Me Do It," *Christianity Today*, October 16, 1987, p. 64.
7. Russell T. Hitt, "Beyond Triumphalism," *Eternity*, September 1986, p. 7.
8. See Ted W. Engstrom with Robert C. Larson, *Integrity* (Waco, Tex.: Word Books, 1987), p. 71.
9. Ibid.
10. McKendree R. Langley, "Televangelism's Crisis, Public Witnesses Future," *Eternity*, June 1987, p. 34.

2. What Star Do We Follow?

1. Karen Burton Mains, "The Way I See It—Resisting the Celebrity Myth," *Today's Christian Woman*, September/October, 1986, p. 96.
2. Mains, p. 2.
3. Carlton Stowers, *Happy Trails: The Story of Roy Rogers and Dale Evans* (Waco, Tex: Word Books, 1979).

4. Dale Evans Rogers with Carole C. Carlson, *Woman, Be All That You Can Be* (Old Tappan: Fleming H. Revell Company, 1980), p. 43.

3. Dangers of Star Gazing

1. Richard Schickel, *Intimate Strangers: The Culture of Celebrity* (New York: Doubleday and Company, 1985), p. 23.
2. Jim Smoke, *Whatever Happened to Ordinary Christians?* (Eugene, Ore.: Harvest House, 1987), pp. 11,12.
3. Ronald Brownstein and Nina Easton, "The New Status Seekers," *Los Angeles Times Magazine*, December 27, 1987, p. 12.
4. See J. I. Packer, *Hot Tub Religion* (Wheaton: Tyndale House Publishers, 1987), pp. 76–79.
5. Richard J. Foster, *Money, Sex and Power* (San Francisco: Harper and Row Publishers, 1985), p. 1.
6. Foster, *Money, Sex and Power*, p. 1.
7. See Dale Evans Rogers with Carole C. Carlson, *Woman, Be All You Can Be* (Old Tappan: Fleming H. Revell Company, 1980), p. 111.

4. The Heritage of Celebrityism

1. Dale Evans Rogers, *Woman, Be All You Can Be* (Old Tappan: Fleming H. Revell Company, 1980), pp. 43–44.
2. See Jon Johnston, *Will Evangelicalism Survive Its Own Popularity?* (Grand Rapids: Zondervan Publishing House, 1980), pp. 123–24. Dr. Johnston also refers to Elizabeth Kaye, "Forever Elvis," *New Times*, November 13, 1978, pp. 36–50; and John Edgerton, "Elvis Lives! The Stuff That Myths Are Made Of," *Progressive*, March 1979, pp. 20–23.
3. Johnston, p. 124.
4. Rick Stanley with Michael K. Haynes, *The Touch of Two Kings* (T2K, 1986), p. 17.
5. Stanley, p. 49.
6. Stanley, p. 83.
7. Stanley, p. 102.
8. Stanley, pp. 106–9.
9. See Sanford Nax, "Bakker Urges Return to American Values," *The Desert Sun* (Palm Springs), February 22, 1988, pt. I, p. 1.
10. "The Jim Bakker Affair," *Christianity Today*, April 17, 1987, p. 37.
11. Louis Sahagun, "Bakkers Return to Desert with Dazzling New Plans," *Los Angeles Times*, February 28, 1988, pt. I, p. 1.
12. According to an Associated Press release from Winston-Salem, North Carolina, "PTL Trustee Seeks to Recover $9.36 Million Paid to Bakkers," *The Daily News* (Los Angeles), Saturday, January 2, 1988, p. 13.
13. See "IRS Withdraws Tax-Exempt Status of PTL Ministry," Associated Press Release, *Los Angeles Times*, April 23, 1988, pt. I, p. 2.
14. Sahagun, "Bakkers Return to Desert with Dazzling New Plans," pt. I, p. 1.
15. Sahagun, p. 1.

16. Kenneth S. Kantzer, "The Road to Restoration," *Christianity Today,* November 20, 1987, p. 19.
17. "The Jim Bakker Affair," *Christianity Today,* April 17, 1987, p. 37.

5. What We Can Learn from Fallen Stars

1. Terry Muck, "The Bakker Tragedy," *Christianity Today,* May 15, 1987, p. 14.
2. Tim LaHaye, *Capital Report,* October 1987, p. 2.
3. *The Banner,* March 21, 1988, p. 6.
4. Muck, "The Bakker Tragedy."
5. Muck, "The Bakker Tragedy."
6. See Kenneth L. Woodward with Frank Gibney, Jr., Patricia Gibney and Partricia King, "The Wages of Sin: How Tough a Penalty for Swaggart?" *Newsweek,* March 7, 1988, p. 51.
7. Associated Press Release, Baton Rouge, La. "Church Leaders Profess Empathy for Confessed Sinner Swaggart," *The Desert Sun,* February 22, 1988, pt. 2, p. 1.
8. "Church Leaders Profess Empathy for Confessed Sinner Swaggart," p. 1.
9. Kenneth L. Woodward with Frank Gibney, Jr., Patricia Gibney and Patricia King, "The Wages of Sin: How Tough a Penalty for Swaggart?" *Newsweek,* March 7, 1988, p. 51.
10. See "Swaggart's Home Council OK's One-Year Ban," *Los Angeles Times,* Saturday, April 2, 1988, pt. 1, p. 20.
11. See Peter H. King, "Swaggart Rejects Terms of Penance, Is Defrocked," *Los Angeles Times,* April 9, 1988, pt. I, p. 1.
12. See Peter H. King, "A Defiant Swaggart Returns to the Pulpit," *Los Angeles Times,* pt. I, p. 1, May 23, 1988.
13. Joanne Kaufman, "The Fall of Jimmy Swaggart," *People Weekly,* March 7, 1988, p. 39.
14. Kaufman, p. 37.
15. Woodward et al., "The Wages of Sin," p. 51.
16. Donald E. Miller, "Sinning Clerics, Public Shame: The Double Indemnity of the Self-Exalted," *Los Angeles Times,* February 26, 1988, pt. 2, p. 7.
17. Miller, "Sinning Clerics," p. 7.
18. Charles Haddon Spurgeon, *The Treasury of David* (New York: Funk & Wagnalls Company, n.d.), p. 324.
19. Jimmy Swaggart, *Straight Answers to Tough Questions* (Brentwood, Tenn.: Wolgemuth and Hyatt Publishers, 1987), p. 132.
20. Swaggart, p. 142.
21. Swaggart, p. 221.
22. Swaggart, p. 223.
23. See John Dart, "A Twist of Fate: Swaggart May Have Been Preaching Against His Own Impulses," *Los Angeles Times,* Saturday, March 5, 1988, pt. 2, p. 6.
24. Dart, "A Twist of Fate."
25. Kaufman, pp. 38, 39.
26. Dart, "A Twist of Fate."

27. Swaggart, *Straight Answers to Tough Questions*, p. 244.
28. Kenneth S. Kantzer, "The Road to Restoration," *Christianity Today*, November 20, 1987, p. 19.
29. Kantzer, p. 21.
30. Kantzer, p. 22.
31. "A Talk With the MacDonalds," *Christianity Today*, July 10, 1987, pp. 38–39.
32. See Pam Hoffman, "Good News for a Fallen Leader," *Christianity Today*, June 17, 1988, p. 65. See also Gordon MacDonald's new book on restoration, *Rebuilding Your Broken World*, Oliver Nelson, A Division of Thomas Nelson Publishers, 1988.
33. "A Talk With the MacDonalds," pp. 38–39.
34. Kantzer, "The Road to Restoration," p. 22.
35. Muck, "The Bakker Tragedy," p. 15.
36. William Shakespeare, "Julius Caesar," act 1, scene 2.
37. Verne Becker, "When a Hero Falls," *University Magazine*, October 1987, p. 32.
38. Jon Johnston, *Will Evangelicalism Survive Its Own Popularity?* (Grand Rapids: Zondervan Publishing House, 1980), p. 70.
39. Johnston, p. 74.

6. Everybody's Somebody in God's Sight

1. Jon Johnston, *Will Evangelicalism Survive Its Own Popularity?* (Grand Rapids: Zondervan Publishing Company, 1980), p. 126.
2. Johnston, p. 126.
3. Johnston, p. 126.
4. Originally stated by English playwright Heathcote Williams, quoted by John Lahr, "Notes on Fame," *Harpers*, January 1978, p. 77. Quoted by Jon Johnston, *Will Evangelicalism Survive Its Own Popularity?* p. 127.
5. Johnston, p. 127.
6. James Dobson, *Hide or Seek* (Old Tappan, N.J.: Fleming H. Revell Company, 1974), p. 24.
7. Don McCrory, "Beneath the Skin," *Eternity*, January 1987, p. 47.
8. See Ralph Blodgett, "America's 'Miss' Speaks on Drugs, Sex, and Faith," *Eternity*, January 1987, p. 47.
9. Lloyd Ogilvie, *Twelve Steps to Living Without Fear* (Waco, Tex.: Word Books, 1987), p. 82.
10. Ogilvie, p. 82.
11. Interview with Rhonda Fleming.
12. Peter E. Gillquist, *Fresh New Insight Into Love Is Now* (Grand Rapids: Zondervan Publishing House, 1970 and 1978), p. 77.
13. Billy Graham, *The Secret of Happiness*, revised and expanded (Waco, Tex.: Word Books, 1985), p. 73.
14. Gillquist, p. 78.
15. Johnston, *Will Evangelicalism Survive Its Own Popularity?* p. 137.

16. See Maurice Wagner, *The Sensation of Being Somebody* (Grand Rapids: Zondervan Publishing House, 1975), pp. 32–37.
17. For thoughts on this passage, I am grateful to an article by Jerry Harvill, "The Search for Significance" *Discipleship Journal*, No. 39, 1987, p. 38.
18. William Barclay, *The Letters to the Corinthians*, *The Daily Study Bible* (Edinburgh: St. Andrew Press, 1954), pp. 39–40.

7. Live—Don't Just Talk—Humility

1. C. Fred Dickason, *Angels, Elect and Evil* (Chicago: Moody Press, 1975), p. 122.
2. Dickason, p. 118.
3. Richard J. Foster, *Money, Sex and Power* (San Francisco: Harper and Row Publishers, 1985), p. 175.
4. Foster, p. 179, 180.
5. Henri Nouwen, *The Genesee Diary* (New York: Image Books, Division of Doubleday & Co., 1981), p. 65.
6. Nouwen, p. 66.
7. See Laurin White, "Humility, The Illusive Virtue," *Discipleship Journal*, No. 24, 1984, p. 33.
8. See William Barclay, *The Gospel of Matthew*, Vol. 1, *The Daily Study Bible* (Edinburgh: St. Andrew Press, 1956), pp. 91–92.
9. Barclay, *The Gospel of Matthew*, Vol. 1, p. 92.
10. Billy Graham, *The Secret of Happiness*, revised and expanded (Waco, Tex.: Word Books, 1985), p. 68.
11. Roy Rogers and Dale Evans, *Happy Trails* (Waco, Tex.: Key-Word Books Publisher, 1979), p. 138.
12. *Happy Trails*, p. 140.
13. *Happy Trails*, p. 159.
14. Graham, p. 78.

8. Buy the Truth and Spend Integrity

1. Verne Becker, "When a Hero Falls," *University*, October 1987, p. 32.
2. Ted W. Engstrom with Robert C. Larson, *Integrity* (Waco, Tex.: Word Books, 1987), p. 10.
3. Jamie Buckingham, "Where Have All the Heroes Gone?" *Charisma*, December 1986, p. 27.
4. Buckingham, p. 28.
5. Buckingham, p. 30.
6. Bruce Larson, *Living on the Growing Edge* (Grand Rapids: Zondervan Publishing House, 1968), p. 112.
7. See Ken Meyers, "I Need a Hero! But I'll Settle for Somebody Famous," *Eternity*, December 1985, p. 39.
8. Daniel J. Boorstin, *The Image or What Happened to the American Dream* (New York: Atheneum, 1962), p. 74.
9. Charles Haddon Spurgeon, *The Treasury of David* (New York: Funk and Wagnalls Company, n. d.), Vol. 5, p. 324.

10. Jane Russell, *An Autobiography, My Paths and My Detours* (New York: Jove Books, 1985), p. 3.
11. Russell, p. 4.
12. See V. Gilbert Beers, "Referee Between Two Loves," *Christianity Today,* April 24, 1986, p. 12.
13. From sermon preached by Clyde Annandale, "Life-Changing Discipline," Evangelical Free Church of Palm Desert, Palm Desert, California, Tape 119.
14. Author interview with Gavin MacLeod.
15. Thomas F. Roeser, "There Is Nothing Worse Than Sin," *Christianity Today,* November 11, 1983, pp. 83–84. This article was reprinted from the *Chicago Sun Times,* August 22, 1983.
16. Alan Bloom, *The Closing of the American Mind* (New York: Simon & Schuster, 1987), pp. 25–26.
17. Bloom, pp. 25–26.
18. Quotations from Secretary Bennett's speech taken from a column by James J. Kilpatrick, ". . . Rights, Wrongs, and Options," United Press Syndicate.
19. ". . . Rights, Wrongs, and Options."
20. Statistics taken from David G. Savage, "High School Test Cheating: 75 Percent Admit It, Cite Pressure," *Los Angeles Times,* Thursday, April 7, 1986, pt. 1, p. 3.
21. John M. Glionna, "Cheating: Just Part of the Game," *The San Diego Tribune,* Monday, November 24, 1988, p. E-1.
22. Information on the meaning of *mensh* based on Leo Rosten, *The Joys of Yiddish* (New York: McGraw-Hill Book Company, 1968), p. 234.

9. Take a Closer Walk with Him

1. The theories of tradition-directed, other-directed and inner-directed people were developed by David Riesman in Leonard Broom and Philip Selznick, *Sociology: A Text With Adapted Readings,* 4th ed. (New York: Harper and Row, 1968), p. 103. Quoted by Jon Johnston, *Will Evangelicalism Survive Its Own Popularity?* p. 105.
2. Ted Koppel made this statement while speaking at the commencement exercises at Duke University in 1987. Reprinted in *Monday Letter,* Evangelical Christian Publishers Association, June 29, 1987.
3. Ronald B. Allen, *Praise! A Matter of Life and Breath* (Nashville: Thomas Nelson, 1980), p. 142.
4. J. I. Packer, *Hot Tub Religion* (Wheaton: Tyndale House Publishers, 1987), p. 85.
5. For this story, I am indebted to Anne Wilcox, "Words of Life, Words of Delight," *Discipleship Journal,* No. 43, 1988, p. 24.
6. David Winter, *Closer Than a Brother* (Wheaton: Harold Shaw Publishers, 1971), p. 6.
7. Adapted from Stuart P. Boehmig, "Steps To Intimacy With God," *Discipleship Journal,* No. 32, 1986, p. 24.
8. Winter, *Closer Than a Brother,* p. 7.
9. Author unknown, quoted by E. Stanley Jones, *Abundant Living* (Nashville: Abbingdon-Cokesbury Press), p. 236.

10. See Warren Myers with Ruth Myers, "The Best Time for Prayer," *Discipleship Journal*, No. 19, 1984, p. 35.

11. Poetry by Kenneth Fearing, quoted by E. Stanley Jones, *Abundant Living* (Nashville: Abingdon-Cokesbury Press, n.d.), p. 234.

12. Penelope J. Stokes, "Toward a Life of Deeper Praise," *Discipleship Journal*, No. 38, 1987, p. 34.

10. Serve the Star, Not the Image

1. Charles Colson, "The Celebrity Illusion," *Christianity Today*, December 11, 1987, p. 72.

2. Jim Smoke, *Whatever Happened to Ordinary Christians?* (Eugene, Ore.: Harvest House, 1987), p. 11.

3. Accounts on Moody and the shoes and Machen and the hot chocolate adapted from Leslie B. Flynn, *The Power of Christlike Living* (Grand Rapids: Zondervan Publishing House, 1962), p. 39.

4. J. Gresham Machen, *Christianity and Liberalism* (Grand Rapids: William B. Eerdmans Publishing Company, 1923), pp. 148–49.

5. See "The Rise and Fall of 'Holy Joe,'" *Time*, August 3, 1987, p. 55.

6. John R. W. Stott, *The Cross of Christ* (Downers Grove: InterVarsity Press, 1986), p. 146.

7. Adapted from Leslie B. Flynn, *The Power of Christlike Living* (Grand Rapids: Zondervan Publishing House, 1962), p. 17.

8. Stott, p. 279.

9. Stott, p. 279.

10. Stott, p. 282.

11. Stott, p. 282. Temple's quote is from his book, *Citizen and Churchman*, p. 74.

12. See Sinclair B. Ferguson, "Where God Looks First," *Eternity*, February 1987, p. 34.

13. See Mark S. Wheeler, "The Marks of a Servant," *Discipleship Journal*, No. 42, 1987, p. 17.

14. Charles Colson, "An Antidote to Christian Bashing," *Christianity Today*, March 4, 1988, p. 64.

15. Author unknown. I found this version, slightly paraphrased, in Barbara Johnson's newsletter, "The Love Line," a publication of Spatula Ministries, Box 444, La Habra, Calif., 90631, April 1988.